THE AUSTRALIANS
HOW THEY LIVE AND WORK

Uniform with this book

The Argentines: How They Live and Work
by Dereck H. N. Foster

The Austrians: How They Live and Work
by Eric Whelpton

The Dutch: How They Live and Work
by Ann Hoffman

The French: How They Live and Work
by Joseph T. Carroll

The Greeks: How They Live and Work
by Brian Dicks

The Irish: How They Live and Work
by Martin Wallace

The Italians: How They Live and Work
by Andrew Bryant

The Spaniards: How They Live and Work
by Michael Perceval

The Swedes: How They Live and Work
by Paul Britten Austin

The West Germans: How They Live and Work
by Reginald Peck

The Australians

HOW THEY LIVE AND WORK

Nancy Learmonth

DAVID & CHARLES : NEWTON ABBOT

ISBN 0 7153 5873 1

LC # 72-89452

Set in 11pt Baskerville, 2pt leaded
and printed in Great Britain by
Latimer Trend & Company Ltd Plymouth
for David & Charles (Holdings) Limited
South Devon House   Newton Abbot   Devon

Contents

INTRODUCTION   9

1   THE COUNTRY AND THE PEOPLE   11
Chief physical characteristics . the first Australians . the
second Australians . the new Australians . national characteristics . historical landmarks

2   HOW THE COUNTRY IS RUN   32
National government . the state parliaments . the voting
system . local government . the public service . commonwealth versus the states . taxation . banking . currency .
the law . parties and policies . defence . external links

3   HOW THE COUNTRY IS MADE UP   58
New South Wales . Victoria . Queensland . South Australia . Western Australia . Tasmania . Internal Territories—Northern Territory . Internal Territories—Australian Capital Territory . External Territories

4   HOW THEY LIVE   70
Housing . urban landscapes . living standards . social
welfare

5   HOW THEY WORK   84
Industry . the power base . iron and steel . other raw
materials . mining and the Australian . other industries .
the rural scene . the wage earner's world . the working
woman . the wider world of trade and tariff

6   HOW THEY LEARN   112
Schools . higher education . the universities . other tertiary
education . adult education . education and society

7   HOW THEY GET ABOUT   124
Air transport . railways . roads . shipping

8   HOW THEY AMUSE THEMSELVES   132
Sport . summer sport . sport in winter . horse racing .
gambling . clubs . paintings . literature . the performing
arts . holidays and festivals . the press . radio and television . censorship

9   HINTS FOR VISITORS   154
Getting there . getting in . getting on . getting about

ACKNOWLEDGEMENTS   161

INDEX   163

List of Illustrations

Cattle being driven across the plains of Western Australia   33
Echo Point, Katoomba, in the Blue Mountains of New South
   Wales   33
Auto header harvesters working on a 9,000 acre wheat crop   34
Part of a mob of about 6,000 merino sheep brought in for
   shearing   34
Canberra, the national capital   51
Sydney from the north   51
A Flying Doctor's plane at work   52
A hydrographer of the Snowy Mountains Hydro Electric
   Project   52
An Aboriginal stockman   85
Aborigines on a hunting expedition   85
Australian Iron and Steel Company works at Port Kembla,
   NSW   86
The Stuart Highway of the Northern Territory   86
Koalas in the koala sanctuary in Queensland   103
A female Great Grey kangaroo with a young 'joey'   103
Australian and Asian students at the University of Western
   Australia   104
A reminder that Australia lies athwart the Tropic of Capri-
   corn (*Photograph Tom Learmonth*)   104

Map
General map of Australia   8

(*All photographs except the last are reproduced by kind permission of Austra-lian News and Information Bureau*)

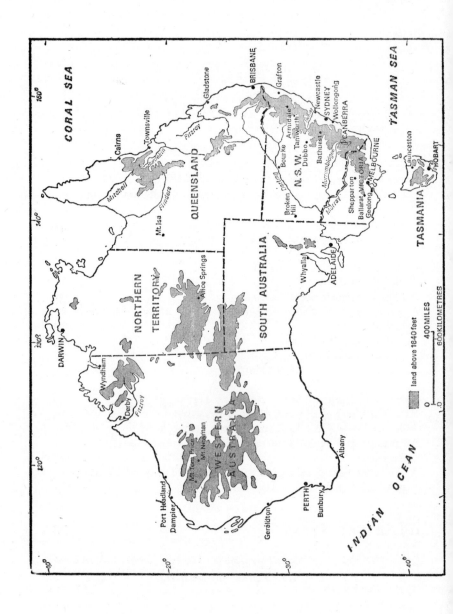

Introduction

THE first official use of the name Australia is found in the correspondence of the Governor of New South Wales in 1817. But some variations of the Latin word *australis* meaning southerly had appeared on charts and in accounts of the region over the previous two centuries.

The Commonwealth of Australia today comprises the six states of New South Wales, Victoria, Queensland, South Australia, Western Australia and Tasmania, and two internal territories, Northern Territory and the Australian Capital Territory. External territories administered by Australia are: Norfolk Island, Papua, the Trust Territory of New Guinea, the Australian Antarctic Territory, the Heard and McDonald Islands, the Cocos (Keeling) Islands and Christmas Island.

Australia is a member of the British Commonwealth, and although ties have loosened and there are voices in favour of republican status, there seems little likelihood of imminent change.

A glance into the writer's bookcase of works on Australia reveals, among many others, the following significant titles: *The Lucky Country*; *The Quiet Continent*; *The Last of Lands*; *The New Australia*. Each points to a separate truth in the make-up and history of the only continent that is a single nation: lucky in its sunshine, in its health and philosophy and economic strength; quiet in its short history far from European battle-grounds; last of the settled continents and unique in its plants and animals; yet new and enthusiastic in its urban and indus-trialised life. Australian society has a remarkable stability, perhaps associated in part with the ease of escape to beach or bush.

The decade of the 1970s will be crucial for Australia. It will show whether the old economy of sheep and wheat can be successfully reorientated towards the new mineral wealth; whether the old alliances will give way to a new independence, even leadership in the Pacific; whether the conservative government that has ruled for close on a quarter of a century will yield to more socialist politics. But whatever party is in power will be faced with many problems: the penetration of foreign capital, the relationships with the neighbouring countries and the intent to maintain a homogeneous population and culture, the apathetic plight of some 140,000 Aborigines; these are just some. To retain its power the government must also have the support of the majority of Australian voters, relaxed and comfortable in their present prosperity and sun-given euphoria.

To find the rounded equivalents for monetary references in the text, add one-fifth to the $A value to get the number of $US; the amount in £ sterling is just under half the number of $A.

I

The Country and the People

THE widespread image of Australia as the land of sunshine is well justified on the whole, for this is the sunniest and driest of continents. But there must be qualifications: in winter Australia claims a greater area of snow cover than Switzerland has, and in summer there are places that get over 100 inches of rain. But the major influence on the climate remains the warm, dry, descending air currents which cover much of the continent much of the time. These are typical of the latitudes, for Australia lies between 12°S and 40°S with the Tropic of Capricorn running right across her wide middle. To the north of the continent are the turbulent atmospheres of the equatorial regions, while to the south lie the cold, stormy latitudes of the 'roaring forties'. Much of the rain Australia gets is brought by invading air masses from these bordering zones.

The northern fringes of the continent have heavy summer downpours, the equivalent of the Asian monsoon but of course in the opposite season; this is the period of the Wet. These rains can sweep far inland, flooding the central deserts. In the south, winter sees a procession of depressions marching from west to east and leaving snow on the high country of Tasmania and the south-east mainland; elsewhere they bring squalls and the 'showers and bright intervals' familiar to the west European, or the people of coastal Washington and British Columbia. Along the eastern margins of the country there can be rain at any season, for the trade winds blow fairly steadily from the vast reservoirs of the Pacific. But the lie of the land, with the high ground close to the coast, prevents this moisture from being carried very far inland. Tully in north-east Queensland has a rainfall average of 179 inches a year; the western margins of Tasmania also average well over 100 inches, but it is spread more evenly over the months and in cooler conditions. Much of central Australia on the other hand averages well below 10 inches, a figure which conceals years and years with no rain at all, followed by a burst of heavy tropical storms. Indeed over almost the whole country the average rainfall figure is deceptive, for the amounts that fall from year to year are wildly unreliable.

Temperatures are a little more predictable: but they often change very rapidly, especially in the south where a heat wave up to and over 95°F (35°C) can be rudely terminated within hours as a 'cool change' sweeps in, lowering temperatures by up to fifteen degrees. The hottest place on record is Marble Bar in Western Australia, which can have as many as 160 days consecutively over 100°F (38°C). Large areas in the centre and west have ninety days or more of this searing heat every summer. The state capitals all lie on the coast and are tempered by sea breezes.

Although a young country in terms of white settlement and economic development, Australia is one of the world's oldest lands physically. The rocks lying beneath the great rolling expanses of the western plateau were once part of the long-foundered continent geologists call Gondwanaland; it linked parts of what are now India, Africa, Australia and Antarctica. Now often masked by desert sands, these rocks contain minerals like gold and nickel. The stony mountain ranges of Arnhem Land, the Kimberleys and Hamersley Ranges, and the bare ridges of central Australia are built of rocks only a little younger. In north-west Western Australia they are now yielding iron ore in quantites enough to feed the world's furnaces for several centuries.

In the vast courses of time, Australia has also been shaped by ice ages: the famous hump of Ayers Rock in the central desert

is made of the huge droppings of an ice sheet, cemented and
then eroded to make one of the world's greatest monoliths. In
later geological eras, seas have lapped the ancient plateaus, and
dried away to leave level strata of ocean deposits: some have
been barely altered since, like the level limestones of the Barkly
Tableland in the north or the unbelievable flatness of the
Nullarbor in the south where the trans-continental railway
runs for 330 miles without a curve. In 1844, the explorer Sturt
set out from Adelaide confident of finding a great inland sea;
he even took a whaleboat. But he was millions of years too late,
and all he found was a monstrous sea of sand-dunes whipped
into waves by the winds of the desert. The deceptive blue expanses still often shown on atlas maps in central Australia are
salt-encrusted lakes, 'infernal seas of mud and brine' as a later
explorer wrote.

The age, mass and simplicity of the western plateau are a
great contrast with the highland belt that girdles the continent
on its eastern side. There the landscapes are much more varied,
etched from a wide variety of rocks: there are the level orange
sandstones of the Blue Mountains, gashed by deep forested
gorges; ancient volcanoes poured out lavas that now form the
fantastic pinnacles of the Warrumbungles or the Glasshouse
Mountains as well as the level plains of western Victoria and
north-east Queensland; hard granites have been weathered
smooth to make the rolling hills of central New South Wales.
Again the atlas map misleads in showing a continuous Great
Dividing Range curving down the east of Australia. The highland zone running 2,500 miles from Cape York to Tasmania
contains a multitude of ranges of all shapes, sizes and directions;
the actual watershed between east and west is generally far
inland of the high mountains. The roof of Australia lies along
the Snowy Mountains in the south-east, where Mount Kos-
ciusko rises 7,316ft, a higher swelling above a massive plateau
well over 6,000ft. It is possible to drive almost to the summit
from the east, but the western approach is much more precipi-
tous.

The rivers that flow east and south from the highlands

are relatively short, about a hundred miles or so; they tumble from the plateaus in spectacular waterfalls, and in flood time spill out over the narrow lowland that fringes the sea. The surf-beaten Pacific coast is edged with an alternation of sandy beaches, rocky headlands, dunes and mangrove-lined estuaries. But the rivers that flow inland from the highlands soon lose heart and many just give up in marshy flats. Australia's only large river system is that of the Murray-Darling, which drains the southern half of the great lowland lying between the western plateau and the eastern highlands. The Murray-Darling basin covers 414,000 square miles, or 14 per cent of Australia. But its average discharge is a third that of the Danube and a tenth that of the Ganges. The basin is comparable with that of the Mississippi but far less useful in soils or climate.

The northern half of the central lowland drains to the Gulf of Carpentaria and has heavy summer rains when the rivers flood; the Dry is very dry. But there are underground sources of water over a large part of the central lowland. Rain from the wet coastal winds seeps through the porous mountain rocks and percolates westwards, trapped between impervious rock layers above and below. In 1887 the first known artesian well was sunk at Thurulgoona in Queensland; it is still flowing. The discovery of the Great Artesian Basin released the pastoralists from dependence on the sporadic river courses; but the water is too saline for irrigation.

The native animals have, of course, inbuilt adaptations to the hazards of their environment; these have not, however, saved them from the depredations of man. The marsupial animals, which carry and suckle their young in pouches, probably came to Australia over a land bridge from south-east Asia in a past era. They include a wide range of creatures, from tiny mice and moles to the magnificent grey and red kangaroos; from the furry koala to the burrowing wombat and the fierce and carnivorous Tasmanian devil. The egg-laying mammals are also unique: the amphibious platypus can be seen in river pools and the spiny ant-eater in the bush. The bird population, being less confined, has a greater overlap with adjoining lands, but Australia has unique species in the flightless cassowary and emu. Less comfortable to contemplate but with some beautiful species are the snakes; about a dozen are dangerous to man when provoked.

The Europeans introduced many plants and animals, most notoriously the rabbit. Before being checked by myxomatosis in the 1950s, they numbered hundreds of millions and had ravaged vast acreages of pasture and crop. Hares, foxes and deer were introduced to provide sport, and of these the fox has become a serious pest. The dingo or wild dog came with the early Aborigines and is a major enemy of the pastoralist; thousands of miles of dingo-proof fences snake across Queensland to exclude them from grazing lands. Wild donkeys descended from draft animals have reached plague proportions in parts of northern Australia. In the far north-west, buffaloes were brought to early settlements and ran wild; today their skins provide an export in leather. Rats came with the convict ships and soon acclimatised. Introduced trout delight anglers in inland waters but not so the predatory European carp.

The first blackberries were carefully cultivated in Tasmania in 1891; now along with the wild rose they are rampant wherever there is settlement and are classed as 'noxious weeds'. The worst plant to escape, however, was the prickly pear, thoughtlessly introduced to provide hedging and stock feed. By 1925 it had smothered over 30 million acres of the Queensland bush and infested a great deal more. The answer, mercifully, was found in the tiny Argentinian moth *Cactoblastis* introduced in 1925; its larvae thrive on prickly pear.

The natural vegetation cover largely reflects the amount of rainfall: a rim of forest runs along the wet eastern hills. Covering some 6 per cent of the country it includes close tropical jungle in Queensland, temperate rain forest farther south and the remnants of great softwood forests in Tasmania. Inland lies the great Australian 'bush'; a term which covers everything from rolling landscapes of trees and pasture in the better watered areas to pincushions of spinifex in seas of desert sand; from the twisted mallee thickets of the south-east and south-west through spindly mulgas to empty desert; and it includes too, the weird northern landscapes of tall anthills and swollen bottle trees. The inland creeks are lined with the evil-smelling gidgee and the straggly coolibah: some maintain that the 'jolly swagman under the shade of the coolibah tree' was written in jest, for the gum tree casts little shade; when the sun is strongest the leaves turn vertically to reduce moisture loss.

The blue haze of so many Australian views is partially caused by the exudations of oil from the ubiquitous eucalypt: over 600 species are known. They are evergreen, yet never green but rather a dull olive-grey; in spring new green shoots give some brightness. But the main harbinger of spring is the brilliant yellow blossom of the wattle, one of the acacia family which, with the eucalypt, dominates the natural vegetation. The oily eucalypt is very inflammable and bush fires a major hazard; yet it is remarkably resilient and within months a blackened stretch of bush will show fresh shoots on the charred trunks.

The idea of conserving a natural heritage which contains so much that is unique has been slow to develop, but is now tugging fairly hard at the Australian conscience. The uniquely grand Great Barrier Reef, threatened with oil exploration, has brought a public reaction strong enough to influence votes; so politicians are slowly beginning to take note. Even so, up to a million kangaroos are shot each year for pet food. The Australian Conservation Foundation (1966) is working hard to provide data as a basis for a rational programme; but there are the inevitable conflicts between short term gain and long term conservation, whether it is in the digging of mineral-rich beach sands or the development of unique alpine areas for hydro-electricity. At least the koala and platypus were saved in time. And although National Parks cover only 1 per cent of the country, they do include representative areas of most of the widely varying environments that are the joy of the continent.

THE FIRST AUSTRALIANS

The Aboriginal people probably reached Australia by a former land link with south-east Asia. Their arrival is estimated to have been spread over a period from 32,000 to 12,000 years ago, following the last ice age. They brought with them only the dingo and their nomadic way of life which depended entirely on what they could hunt or gather. Survival depended on a very thorough understanding of their environment, and they were really the first conservationists, for to destroy that environment meant starvation. Their migrations followed the seed time of grasses and the fruiting of trees and shrubs, the movements of fish and even of moths which took the tribes up to the high summer pastures. Kangaroo and wallaby were hunted by spear and throwing-stick; these sticks did not return to the thrower like the boomerang, that fascinating aero-dynamic discovery the Aborigines kept only as a toy for their amusement. Game was flushed out by fire; but although widespread bushfires clearly affected the vegetation long before the white man came they were modest effects compared with those wrought by two centuries of European occupance. Only a few hundred Aborigines still follow the old tribal way of life out of contact with the white man.

Physically, the full blood Aborigine has a very black skin, black hair that is curly not frizzy, a sloping forehead with large brow ridges, a protruding jaw and a wide flat nose. There were regional variations, for instance more negrito types were found in Queensland and in Tasmania, where they have long been extinct. The racial association is with tribal people still found in south India and in Ceylon and south-east Asia. But with long isolation the Australian Aborigines developed distinctive features.

They have no written language, but some 500 regional languages probably existed at the time of first European contact; they were mainly agglutinative, that is, elements were

B

added to express more complex meanings. Culture and religion were closely linked with the way of life: complex kinship rules preserved the race, while destroying unwanted or unhealthy lives. The objects of worship were natural features like a hill or stream or tree; the sacred *tjuringa* was a rounded piece of wood or stone which would become the dwelling place of its owner's soul after death, and it was carefully secreted in a sacred place.

When European settlement began in 1788, there were some 300,000 Aborigines, and Captain Phillip was instructed to 'conciliate their affections and to enjoin all subjects to live in amity and kindness with them'. But there was too great a gulf in culture and comprehension between the races; and in any case the settlers wanted and needed the land. In 1966 there were 79,620 Aborigines of more than 50 per cent Aboriginal blood; probably about half of that number genuinely full blood. In the 1971 census for the first time Aborigines were included in the totals and not made a separate entry. They are increasing in numbers after a long decline. For long they were considered a dying race, an attitude that conditioned the white man's approach, whether he was a ruthless pioneer or a well-meaning official.

Of a total today of some 140,000 who consider themselves Aborigines, about 45,000 live on remote, barren tribal reserves. Their living conditions are primitive and they have an infant death rate ten times that of white Australians. A further 70,000 dwell in crude shacks on the fringes of outback country towns; they depend on unskilled and seasonal labour and their easy-going ways bring the contempt of the white citizens. The remaining small minority live in the cities where alone the government policy of assimilation might have some meaning as they painfully climb the social and economic ladder. Only 2 per cent of the children qualify for higher schooling and barely a handful have reached tertiary education.

Aboriginal affairs are handled by a Commonwealth Ministry which also includes tourism, the environment and the arts among its concerns. In the states there is widespread discrimination, most severe in Queensland. Aboriginal stockmen are the mainstay of the cattle industry in the tropical north. In the 1960s the Gurindji people attempted unsuccessfully to resume their old tribal lands now included in a large foreign-owned cattle station; they wanted to work it on their own behalf. The coming of the new mineral era has brought the issue of Aboriginal land rights to a head. The Yirrkala people of Arnhem Land sought through the courts to restrain a firm about to exploit the bauxites of their old tribal territory on Gove Peninsula. After two years a historic judgement was made in the Supreme Court of the Northern Territory in January 1972 in the following words:

> *The doctrine of communal native title has no place in common law. On the foundation of a colony, native title to land was only recognised pursuant to legislative or executive action, and since all Northern Territory was Crown property a person had to show title from the Crown which the Aboriginals of Yirrkala had failed to do. Although they had a system of law their relationship with the land was not sufficiently economic to amount to a proprietary interest.*

An appeal to the Prime Minister brought the final rejection of any Aboriginal land rights. They may be granted fifty year leases of the lands they have occupied for centuries, but the government retains all mineral and forestry rights. They must learn to assimilate with the rest of Australians. Although money is promised for Aboriginal improvement, there has been a sharp reaction among the younger and more articulate. And on 26 January 1972 they marked the Prime Minister's announcement and the anniversary of the first white settlement by setting up a tented 'Aboriginal Embassy' on the lawns opposite Parliament House, claiming that they are aliens in their own land.

The average well meaning white Australian feels some sense of guilt over the plight of these dark people but is at a loss over how it can best be alleviated. In 1967 an overwhelming majority voted to amend the constitution so that Aborigines could be included in the census totals and their affairs be brought more within the powers of the central governn Aborigines have had voting rights since 1962; officially, r tive drinking laws are disappearing. Equal wages with white workers are statutory but often ignored. For instance, on cattle stations the stockmen are often paid a low cash wage supplemented by rations which keep a large collection of dependents.

Apart from rich traditions and cultures of their own past, the Aborigines have produced artists acclaimed by European standards, notably Namatjira, and a fine poet in Kath Walker. They have produced a number of sporting personalities like Lionel Rose and Evonne Goolagong, voted Australian of the Year in 1972. But the thinking Aborigine is very conscious of the dilemmas facing his people today and of a considerable frustration which is beginning to find some militant leadership rather pathetically aping North American black militant groups. To him the present assimilation policy spells second class citizenship; he seeks instead some racial and cultural identity but with equality of opportunity with the white Australians.

THE SECOND AUSTRALIANS

European settlement in Australia began with the arrival of what afterwards came to be known as the First Fleet, in 1788. The fleet comprised eleven small sailing ships with a combined tonnage considerably less than a modest steamer of today; it had battled some 15,000 miles from England via Rio de Janeiro and the Cape of Good Hope with a very mixed cargo indeed. Of some 1,450 souls, 750 were convicts and the rest sailors and military. There is a more accurate record of the livestock: 7 horses, 48 sheep and goats, 74 swine, 291 assorted poultry, 5 rabbits, 5 cows and 2 bulls.

Much has been made of the convict origins of Australia. But, in fact, over the period of transportation which ended in the 1850s (save to Western Australia), a total of about 165,000 convicts were sent out as involuntary settlers, while from 1825 to 1850 there were 223,000 free migrants. Few of the convicts in the nature of things were in any position to found families in Australia, so that the proportion of today's population descended from them is minute, though such ancestry is now claimed with some relish. The bulk of the convicts were a pretty rough lot, in spite of widespread beliefs that they were the victims of a vicious penal system who had committed but trivial crimes. True, they were the drop-outs of a ruthless and industrialising society; but only a small proportion were transported for really petty offences and a few more for the 'gentleman's crime' of forgery; there were some political exiles like the Tolpuddle Martyrs convicted for precocious union activity.

Many convicts, having served their time, were emancipated and settled in Australia; they came to form an important group in the early days of the colony. Free settlement began slowly, with merchants and officers who acquired land. But the flow from England increased with the news of good inland pastures and became a flood when gold was discovered in the 1850s: the population trebled from 40,000 to 110,000 in the period 1851–61. Chinese came first as shepherds but soon also sought the gold-fields and sent home for their relatives. They were disliked for their industry and clannishness and laws were introduced to exclude them; the first seeds of the White Australia policy were sown in the gold-fields. When the gold rush faded, immigration tailed off and by 1870 the native-born Australians outnumbered immigrants. By 1914 only 11 per cent of the population had been born outside Australia. At this time about a fifth of the population were descended from Irish Catholic migrants; they have kept alive, if now fairly diluted, some of the distrust and animosity which remain the horror of Ireland in the 1970s. Other groups are the result of 'chain migrations' from particular valleys or villages in Europe when whole families followed each other out to new irrigation areas for instance. The Lutherans who settled in South Australia in 1842 were the founders of a distinctive life and landscape of trim vineyards and Teutonic order. But the great bulk of migrants were British and they ensured a British pattern on the Australian way of life which still persists despite its steadily growing distinctiveness.

THE NEW AUSTRALIANS

The severe economic depression of the 1930s reduced the birth rate, so that the numbers entering the work force after World War II were too low for economic growth. The war had also brought home to Australians the vulnerable military position of their country as a sparsely peopled continent with a western culture set at the edge of a teeming Asian continent. So in 1947 a campaign was launched under the Labor government then in power to increase the population by 1 per cent per year through sponsored migration. Labor had previously been hostile to immigration schemes, fearing job competition; a similar dread of cheap labour was behind their devotion to the White Australia policy. (Labor, as an Australian political party, is always spelt in the American way, perhaps because Australian socialism owed much to American writings.)

The first of the 'new Australians' were refugees and displaced persons from the many camps in Europe; 'reffos' the Australians called them at first but the term New Australians was officially encouraged to give a better image to the campaign. Assisted passages for British migrants were subsidised by both Australian and British governments; the cost per adult was only £10.00 ($A21.50, $US26.00). Of a total of 1,719,000 migrants who came and stayed between 1947 and 1966, some 40 per cent were British, 15 per cent from other north European countries, 15 per cent from east Europe and 27 per cent from southern Europe.

The strong Anglo-Saxon dominance of the racial stock was modified and by 1966 about 20 per cent of the population was non-British in origin. The immigrants were an invaluable mobile work force; though largely unskilled they were adaptable and made a useful contribution to the economy. Over 80 per cent settled in the towns, however, adding to the urbanisation which has been a feature of Australia since the first colonies were established round the port capitals. Ethnic groups have tended to stay together in the bigger towns, but the second generation rapidly assimilates and in turn brings the parents more fully into the Australian way of life.

There are still a number of lonely, elderly migrants, those who came in the first post-war waves as young bachelors and who have never really been absorbed. Paradoxically, however, the biggest return of migrants to their homelands has been among the British and New Zealand groups. There is a lot of debate as to why this is so. Many Australians affect scorn of the 'whingeing Pom' who refuses to settle and is lost without the alleged cotton wool environment of his welfare state. But a family with a chronically sick member can be forgiven for longing for a national health service which saves him from the crippling financial burden this can represent in Australia. Perhaps some other causes for migrant discontent will emerge from later chapters. But on balance, the great majority settle down happily and, like many converts, become even more enthusiastic than those born to their beliefs.

The 1970s are likely to see a falling off in the European migration. Official campaigns are still quite vigorous, but the annual quota of British migrants was reduced from 170,000 to 140,000 in 1971. And in 1972 the British government withdrew from the assisted passages scheme. There has been an increasing flow of migrants from the United States to Australia; in 1970 there were 4,565 arrivals and 1,191 departures of permanent settlers. There is a feeling in Australia that the time has come to pause and consolidate; and to examine whether the migrant's economic contribution is now enough to justify the costs of educating and housing his family. There is more emphasis on quality than quantity in potential migrants, and current propaganda pays more attention to 'finding out the facts' while still emphasising the rewards of the life to be lived down under.

The White Australia policy has been officially expunged from party political platforms. At the same time it is the clear intent to maintain a homogeneous and predominantly European population. Present restrictions effectively preclude all but highly skilled and educated Asians. The Labor Party is committed to further liberalisation of the laws to admit more Asians but they will never be more than a selected minority.

NATIONAL CHARACTERISTICS

It has become a truism to say that the Australian is largely a city dweller: of a population of 12,728,461 in 1971, over 80 per cent lived in half a dozen large coastal cities. Most of the rest lived within fifty miles of the sea in a belt stretching from Geraldton in Western Australia round the south-west and south-east margins of the country and north to Cairns in Queensland. Even within this narrow rim there are large empty areas, like the Nullarbor Plains.

A dense rural population in Australia is sixteen per sq mile: in monsoon Asia a square mile often has to support 400 people and in north-west Europe over sixty. In North America on the other hand 'close' rural settlement would be between thirty and forty per square mile. Large hunks of Australian have their population densities described in square miles per person, like Diamantina Shire in south-west Queensland with some 300 people in 36,560 square miles. The rural areas are steadily losing people to the cities, a trend likely to speed up if the rural recession continues.

It is with trepidation that one would depict a 'typical' Australian, but if such exists, he would be a suburban dweller who travels by car to work during the week and to beach or bush at the weekend. The tall, bronzed and lean type like the youthful Chips Rafferty can be found of course, riding a horse round the outback, but he is much rarer than the rather sleek and well fed office worker, tending to a paunch in middle life. On the other hand the widely held image of the rather aggressive Australian has some truth in it.

The majority put down Christianity as their religion, although only one in five attends church services. Some 38 per cent describe themselves as Anglican, 30 per cent as Roman Catholic, 12 per cent as Methodist and 10 per cent as Presbyterian. While the number of Roman Catholics shows increase, there is also a growing number declaring no religious belief.

The Australian language and accent are remarkably homogeneous, transcending social and geographical barriers; there is only a mildly increasing refinement with education. Derived originally from the dialects of the first settlers, Australian English has many distinctive words stemming from other sources. Aboriginal names appear in place names, plant and animal names: Wagga Wagga is a major inland town of New South Wales, coolibah and gidgee are two of the innumerable tree names, kookaburra and budgerigar, kangaroo and wallaby among examples of animals and birds. American influences in the ninteenth century left words associated with land tenure, like block or selection. Standard English words have different connotations in Australia: a station is a rural property, a paddock any field, a mob is a flock of sheep and so on. Other words, long forgotten in England, include larrikin, a young street rowdy, and a ringer, one of the shearing team. The flat tone and wide vowel sounds of the Australian accent are unmistakeable. The Queenslander may talk more slowly as befits the hot climate, and the West Australian with a particularly rapid and careless patois, but there is little national variation.

The 'typical' Australian has a gift of improvisation, a legacy of pioneering necessity as the mother of mechanical invention. Important innovations include the 'stump-jump' plough and the stripper harvester. From the same origins come the readiness to help anyone in trouble and the genuine spirit of 'mateship'. Loyalty within a group of friends is very important. He is convinced that he does indeed live in God's Own Country and takes unkindly to any criticism of it. While much less suspicious of the newcomer than in the past, he wants to see him settle down as quickly as possible, to loosen his old ties and to become a 'dinkum Aussie'.

HISTORICAL LANDMARKS

The north coast of Australia was known to Asian traders long before the first documented European sighting in 1606, when a Dutch ship sailed down the western side of Cape York. Portuguese navigators had almost certainly also made earlier landfalls in the sixteenth century. During the seventeenth century further landings were made along the west coast by ships making for the Indies: they crossed the Indian Ocean before the westerlies, and must have often seen the Australian coast before turning north with the trade winds. In 1616 a Dutch sailor, Dirk Hartog, nailed a pewter plate to a post on a sandy island that now bears his name; now in Amsterdam the plate is the oldest European relic from Australia. In 1642 Abel Tasman was sent to look for new trading lands from the Dutch settlement at Batavia in Java. Sailing east along the southern margins of the continent he discovered the island of Tasmania, though the name he gave it was Van Diemen's Land, after the Dutch Governor at Batavia; he sailed on to discover New Zealand. An English buccaneer, William Dampier, had a look at the northern coast of Western Australia in 1688; his published report and a subsequent expedition merely confirmed that this seemed a useless land of heat and flies and miserable natives. So Australia was left to its Aborigines for another century.

The expansion of trade and the need for raw materials in a maritime age brought renewed interest in the 'Southland' in the eighteenth century. In 1770, Captain James Cook sailed west from Tahiti under sealed orders to look for new lands. He rediscovered New Zealand and was making for Van Diemen's Land when his ship was edged northwards by the Pacific swell. And on 20 April he made landfall on the green south-east tip of Australia. The full shape and size of the continent was not to be established until the 1840s. It was thought that the 'New Holland' of the western discoveries was separated from New South Wales by a stretch of sea.

Meanwhile European settlement had begun when the colony of New South Wales was declared on 26 January 1788; the first settlement lay on the shore of Port Jackson, a few miles north of the Botany Bay Cook had found. The tiny, isolated colony faced starvation in its first two years, but within decades was emerging from a gaol to an established community. It was ruled by a series of military governors who included Bligh, famed for his earlier and incredible voyage in an open boat from the mutineering *Bounty*, and Lachlan Macquarie, a dour and devoted Scot with vision and enterprise who is commemorated in place names all over Australia. The officers of the garrison became very powerful in their control of all exchange and trade; rum was virtually a currency. They demanded land and convict labour to work it; along with the first free settlers, merchants and emancipated convicts they pushed back the frontiers of settlement. The Blue Mountains that had hemmed in the colony were first crossed in 1813 and soon the flocks and herds were fanning out over the western slopes.

Charles Sturt solved the problems of the river system by sailing right to the mouth of the Murray in 1829. Thomas Mitchell had meantime discovered the 'boundless plains' along the Darling, and the overlanders from New South Wales literally followed in the tracks of his drays when he explored the lush green lands of western Victoria. But here they found some hardy Vandiemonians already in occupation along the coast. No legislation could control the flood of 'squatters' whose lives were the stuff of pioneering: crude slab huts were put up by waterholes and the sheep allowed to graze freely under the supervision of convict shepherds. The Aborigines were ruthlessly dispossessed and the Squatters became a most powerful group in the colony, gaining some legal security of tenure by the 1840s.

The basis of their wealth was the merino sheep, a breed well-adapted to Australian conditions by its Spanish origins; it was introduced in 1797. Wool provided a valuable and non-perishable export that soon became the basis of the economy; and until the present decade, Australia has continued ever since to 'ride on the sheep's back'.

Offshoots of the New South Wales settlement were made at Hobart in 1804 and at Moreton Bay in 1821; these became the nuclei of Tasmania and Queensland respectively. Another at Port Phillip on the south coast and the colony of Victoria was not established until the 1830s. Western Australia began with a military garrison at Albany in 1826, superseded by a free settlement on the Swan River in 1829. South Australia was also a free settlement born of Gibbon Wakefield's theories: land was sold at a reasonable price and the money used to bring out men to work it. Three military garrisons were set up at different times in the far north in the 1820s and 1830s, to thwart suspected French interest in the continent, but permanent settlement did not begin until the Northern Territory was established in 1868.

The first generation of native-born Australians soon felt restive at the remote, insensitive and bureaucratic control from London, 12,000 miles and many months away. Locally there was also antagonism between the growing urban proletariat and the wealthy Squatters; this was especially over the continuation of transportation. Convicts were a source of labour, but were felt as a blot and impediment to a growing nation. Transportation to eastern Australia ceased in 1852; it was ludicrous to send criminals to a land where gold was being discovered over a wide belt through New South Wales and Victoria.

The gold rush era marked a new stage. Population trebled and when the first easy diggings gave way to deeper mining needing capital, the 'diggers' turned to the land. But by now it was locked firmly in the hands of the Squatters, and only a series of Land Acts released some for the new settlers, who were known as Selectors. But the attempts at bringing about closer settlement were largely a failure, partly through abuse of the system, partly through ignorance of farming, but mainly because much of Australia is unsuited for small scale farming; dreams of an English landscape emerging with neat villages, trim hedges and fields soon perished in the harsh realities of drought and flood.

Many more of the diggers settled in the towns and became a political force that led to rapid constitutional development. The incident of the skirmish at Eureka Stockade at Ballarat in 1854, when miners, infuriated by red tape and corruption, barricaded themselves against the troopers, has become part of the Australian legend. It expressed something of the rugged resentment of authority that still marks the national character.

By the 1850s the six settlements had developed into separate colonies and, with the exception of Western Australia, had their own constitutions and parliaments. Some were to make important political innovations long before the mother country, like the secret ballot and votes for women. The rivalry that developed between them has left legacies still affecting Australia. Each of the port capitals for instance cast a rail net into the hinterland to trawl in produce for export; they used varying gauges which inhibited inter-state trading after federation. The scramble for the products of the Murray Valley led to frontier tariff barriers bisecting the basin, and the waters of the country's only big river system are still a source of controversy between three states.

Although moves towards federation had been made sporadically from the 1840s, it was not until the closing decades of the century that the debate became real. Impetus came from the growing need for a unified approach to problems of external defence and internal trade. Of the two richest colonies, Victoria, which had industrialised behind strong protectionist policies, advocated federation; New South Wales, devoted to free trade, was less enthusiastic. Queensland used her promised support to gain advantages for her sugar trade, and Western Australia wrung the promise of a transcontinental railway from the bargain.

The Commonwealth of Australia came into being on 1 January 1901. There had already begun a surge of nationalism fostered by the *Bulletin*. The rural economy was being strengthened by the development of wheat strains by Farrer, the introduction of refrigeration and the expansion of irrigation. Trade Unionism gathered force in the factory sweat shops of Victoria, among the shearing gangs that followed the fleece and along the busy waterfronts. From it the Australian Labor Party emerged as the political wing.

But for many, the real birth of the nation came with World War I, when 60,000 Australians died fighting for the 'old country'. Between the wars, however, Australia seemed to turn in on herself again, only to be brought forcibly to recognise her dependence on the world outside by the great economic depression of the 1920s and 1930s which robbed her of markets and of foreign capital. At one time a third of the work force was unemployed. Drastic action followed the acceptance of the Premiers' Plan in 1931 for severe retrenchment, followed by devaluation, reduced wages and imports. The country recovered rather more rapidly than many in re-establishing her trade.

The outbreak of World War II found Australia once more fully committed to support Britain. This time she was more intimately involved, for the Japanese advanced almost to the northern gates. In 1942 Darwin was bombed, but the same year saw the turning point of the war in the air-battle over the Coral Sea, which deterred the Japanese invasion of southern New Guinea. Before the atomic bombs ended the war in the Pacific, Australia had lost some 30,000 men and many thousands had suffered in prison camps.

Australians had learned painfully that old links were not enough and had turned to America for support in her defence; there had been some bitterness between the Australian and British governments over the re-deployment of Australian troops from North Africa. The growing alliance with America led to Australian involvement in Vietnam, which has been a source of controversy and a drain on resources. The present network of pacts and alliances is more fully described in Chapter 2.

Meantime a post-war Labor government under Chifley had widely extended social services and initiated the immigration campaign. In 1949 Labor was replaced by a coalition of the essentially conservative Liberal Party with the Country Party, which remains in power at the time of writing. The period since 1945 has seen great industrial expansion, the achievement of the gigantic Snowy Mountains Hydro-Electric Scheme, irrigation developments and a growth in population to over 12 millions. Most important of all, it has seen the discovery at breath-taking rate of enormous quantities of minerals that are in demand in all industrial countries. The significance of these discoveries in their importance to Australia today has been likened to the effects of that first great break-through which the infant colony of New South Wales made in crossing the barrier of the Blue Mountains 150 years earlier.

2

How the Country is Run

SINCE 1901 Australia has had a federal form of government resulting from the voluntary union of the former British colonies of New South Wales, Tasmania, Victoria, Queensland, South Australia and Western Australia. These became states within the new Commonwealth of Australia and retained their parliaments, judiciary and public services. The two internal territories do not have separate responsible government but each sends a representative to the Commonwealth Parliament. The term Commonwealth is a little confusing at first to the British incomer, accustomed to think of the word only in

---

Australia is a continent of contrasts. The top illustration is typical of the north and central areas where cattle often have to travel hundreds of miles to railheads or seaports. These cattle are being driven across Anna Plains inland from Broome in the north-east of Western Australia.

Very different is the scenery of the Lookout at Echo Point, Katoomba, more than 3,000ft up in the Blue Mountains of New South Wales. Here the cliff falls 600ft sheer into Jamieson Valley. The rock formation is called the Three Sisters.

reference to the British Commonwealth of Nations. The realities of a federal system are also strange to him, but are much more familiar to the American or West German. The co-existence of two sets of statutes is soon evident: defence, postal services and income tax for instance are controlled from the centre, while police, education and censorship are among the responsibilities of the individual states.

The federal fathers who drafted the constitution had the benefit of much precedent to study, from Switzerland to the United States. In addition they had a strong heritage of British parliamentary practice already incorporated in the colonial constitutions. The result was a fascinating compromise between the two streams, which has some anomalies but on the whole makes a fluid working arrangement suited to the needs of a continent-country.

The Commonwealth Parliament consists of two houses: the lower house is called the House of Representatives and the upper house is the Senate. The House of Representatives has a maximum life of three years and is elected by universal adult franchise of British subjects. ('British subject' covers the people of all member states of the British Commonwealth of Nations; in Australia the term is often clarified by the definition 'British

———

Auto header harvesters move in formation to take a giant slice out of a 9,000 acre wheat crop. Widespread drought in 1967–8 cut production to only 277,000,000 bushels from the previous year's record crop of 467,000,000 bushels; but favourable seasonal conditions and increased plantings have reversed the decline and production is again soaring.

A section of a mob of about 6,000 merino sheep being brought in from the back paddocks of the shearing shed on a sheep station.

C

subject-Australian citizen'.) The number of Members of the House of Representatives or MHRs must, by the constitution, be as nearly as possible double the number of Senators. The Senate was set up initially to be the custodian of the rights and interests of the states, and has ten members from each, regardless of size. Its lifetime is six years, but five Senators retire from each state every three years. Elections for the two houses are therefore frequently out of phase.

Each of the Representatives in the lower house is sent by an electorate of which the boundaries are drawn, in the words of the *Official Yearbook of the Commonwealth of Australia* (*1971*), 'on a quota basis, but taking into account community interests, means of communication, physical features, existing boundaries and other factors'. The number of electorates in each state are: New South Wales 45; Victoria 34; Queensland 18; South Australia 12; Western Australia 9; Tasmania 5. The five Tasmanian MHRs are the minimum laid down by the constitution and more than would be justified by her size or population. Redistribution of electoral boundaries after each census is required by the Electoral Act, but has at times been evaded or postponed in pursuit of vested political interests.

The House of Representatives has a Speaker and the Senate a President, both in the British tradition expected to be 'above the battle'. Government is essentially by Cabinet, again on the British model, and unlike the US presidential system of executive leadership with considerable power invested in President and Governors, and with no member of the executive having a seat on the legislative body. Cabinet members are chosen from among his Ministers by the Prime Minister, who is Leader of the political party in power. At present the Cabinet comprises thirteen members chosen from twenty-six Ministers, any of whom may attend meetings when their own Departments are involved. A federal Executive Council was established as a purely formal body comprising all the Ministers and presided over by the Governor General.

There is no constitutional basis for the political parties,

which are private and autonomous organizations, with party alignments running through and dominating both houses, whose rules on admission of members, drafting of policies and choice of candidates are their own affair and in no way enforceable through the courts. The widely practised system in the USA of holding direct primaries (state controlled election of party candidates by registered party members) is not used in Australia. The Senate is the house of review, and it cannot indefinitely block legislation stemming from the lower house. In the event of a deadlock, if the Senate twice rejects or unacceptably amends a bill from the House of Representatives, the Governor-General can resolve it by a double dissolution of both houses, followed by elections. This has happened twice since federation. There is machinery for resolving further deadlock through convening a joint session of both houses and accepting an absolute majority decision.

The Governor-General is the representative of the Crown in Australia and is appointed by the ruling British monarch on the advice of the Australian Prime Minister. It is unlikely that any but an Australian will be appointed in future, although prior to Lord Casey's term (1965-9) there had been only two Australian Governors-General. The former practice of appointing distinguished Britons brought some dedicated service but is now counter to Australian sentiments and rightly so. The present Governor-General is Sir Paul Hasluck, an eminent statesman and a West Australian. The Governor-General has some residual powers under the constitution, notably the right to dissolve Parliament. Acting for the Queen, he gives assent to Acts as a formality. He makes the official declarations of war (and peace) and is the conventional head of the executive and the armed forces.

The constitution is interpreted and safeguarded, in case of dispute, by the totally independent High Court created by the constitution primarily for this purpose and, like the US Supreme Court, designed to stand above both state and federal authorities; its justices are appointed by the Commonwealth Parliament. The High Court has played a vital part in the evolution of government in Australia, particularly in the relative power of the central and state parliaments. In general, decisions have trended towards increased Commonwealth and weakened state power. It has made important, far reaching judgements: in 1948–9 the Labor Party's proposed legislation to abolish all non-government banks was held to be invalid. In 1942, the High Court upheld the priority of the newly imposed federal income tax over state income tax. In 1950 the Liberal/Country Party coalition sought to dissolve the Australian Communist Party, but the Act was held to be invalid by the High Court. The ultimate recourse to the Privy Council in London on federal matters was abolished in 1968: it had rarely been used.

The constitution can only be amended by a national referendum based on the electoral franchise. The proposal must be approved by a majority of voters and in a majority (at least four) of the states. Since federation twenty-six such proposed amendments have been put to this test; the electors have only assented to five of them. The first, in 1906, related to the election of Senators; two others (1910 and 1928) to the assumption of state debts by the Commonwealth; one was accepted in 1947 in respect of extending social services; and the latest, in 1967, related to Aborigines as described on p 19. The 1967 referendum had two parts: the second sought to break the fixed relationship between numbers of MHRs and Senators to allow for an increase of the lower house alone. This the Australian voter rejected, seeing it as a device to create more politicians.

The powers invested in the Commonwealth are best indicated by the following list of Ministers: Prime Minister; Trade and Industry; Foreign Affairs; Primary Industry; Postmaster General; Treasurer; Shipping and Transport; Supply; Defence; National Development; Labour and National Service; Education and Science; Interior; External Territories; Health; Housing; Immigration; Social Services; Works; Civil Aviation; Customs and Excise; Environment, Aborigines and the Arts; Attorney-General; Repatriation; Army; Navy; Air. Their functions are covered under some forty headings in the constitution detailing the spheres in which the Commonwealth may make laws. But the central government only has *exclusive* control of defence, customs and excise (including currency and coinage), foreign affairs, the territories and the Commonwealth public service.

On all other topics the states may also pass laws. But a valid Commonwealth law is paramount in the event of any inconsistency. Section 51 of the constitution also gives the Commonwealth power to legislate in some matters which it has only recently taken up, for instance in relation to divorce and matrimony and parental rights and custody of children. The Commonwealth took an early hand in arbitration and industrial relations. The prickliest of all the provisions of the constitution has turned out to be Section 92: 'trade, commerce and intercourse among the states shall be completely free'. The interpretations of this section have had far-reaching effects on the development of transport, as described in Chapter 7.

THE STATE PARLIAMENTS

Each state has a Governor representing the Crown; here, too, there is a growing tendency to appoint an Australian, though a number are still British. The states abrogated many powers at federation but their parliaments, like the governments in individual states of the USA, still play a very important part in the rules and regulations that affect the everyday lives of their citizens. Police, education, licences, land policy, mining laws, road safety and local government are among their responsibilities. Inter-state anomolies in censorship or gambling laws can be comic; but differences in education systems can be a serious nuisance.

Queensland has only had a lower house since 1922; it is called the Legislative Assembly. This is also the name of the lower house in New South Wales, Victoria and Western Australia. The lower house in Tasmania and South Australia is the House of Assembly. The Tasmanian House of Assembly has a life of five years, the others three years. All are elected on the same adult franchise as the Commonwealth House of Representatives. The chief minister is called the Premier.

The upper houses are all known as Legislative Councils, but differ in franchise. The universal adult franchise applies in Victoria, Western Australia and Tasmania; a property qualification applies in South Australia. In New South Wales the Legislative Council is elected by both houses sitting together. The periods of life also vary between states.

THE VOTING SYSTEM

Australia was ahead of Britain in a number of electoral innovations: universal adult suffrage (implying votes for women) was first introduced in South Australia in 1894 and in all states by 1909, while it was not achieved in the mother country until 1928. South Australia and Victoria had the secret ballot (still sometimes referred to in the USA as the Australian ballot) in 1856, and New South Wales and Tasmania were only two years behind; it dates only from 1872 in Britain. The principle of the 'Australian ballot' was adopted in Massachusetts, USA, in 1888 and other American states followed suit during the next fifteen years. All the states paid their members by 1900 and the Commonwealth since its inception; payment began in Britain in 1911. Further innovations include the compulsory registration of voters, compulsory and preferential voting.

Compulsory voting was introduced in 1924 for both Commonwealth and state elections. Enrolment of voters is compulsory and a fine is likely for those who, once enrolled, fail to show 'good cause' for not voting. This compulsion comes as a shock to the American, the Britisher or New Zealander. Its blessings are, to say the least, mixed. It guarantees a high polling rate, of course, but taking the horse to the water does not necessarily ensure his health. There are always a good many spoiled ballot papers, officially recorded as 'informal votes'. And coupled with the system of preferential voting described below, it leads to the so called 'donkey vote' in which the disinterested, the disenchanted and the just plain stupid among the electorate simply number their preferences straight down the ballot paper. Since the candidates' names are printed in alphabetical order this can have predictable results; it pays a party to choose an Anderson as against a Young to represent them!

Preferential voting applies to all the states and was introduced for Commonwealth elections in 1918. Electors must number the candidates in order of preference. A candidate having an absolute majority of 'first preferences' wins, of course. If there is not one, then the candidate with the lowest number of first preferences is eliminated; the 'second preferences' given by his supporters are then allocated as if they were first preferences to the relevant candidates. If this still fails to produce an absolute majority, that is half plus one of the valid votes at least, the procedure is repeated with the elimination of the candidate having the second lowest number of first preferences and the redistribution of his supporters' second preferences, and so on. The eventual winner may not have held the lead originally in first preferences, but is considered to be more representative of the will of the electorate as a whole than the winner often is in a British or US election who, while 'first past the post', may in fact have a minority of the total votes cast. Quite often the winning candidate is the one most widely placed as a second preference. This is a fact not lost on the party canvassers who thrust their unofficial guides on 'how to vote' into the electors' hands as they enter the polling booths. The preferential system also leads to victories by candidates for the smaller parties, notably the Country Party, since many voters both Liberal and Labor place the Country Party man as a second preference rather than risk that their second preferences might help a main party candidate to power. Voting machines are not used, and would probably be unacceptable to Australians.

LOCAL GOVERNMENT

For purposes of local government the more closely settled areas of the large states and the whole of Tasmania and Victoria are divided into smaller units having names that vary with the states. In New South Wales they are cities, municipalities and shires all with councils elected on the parliamentary franchise. In Victoria they are cities, towns, boroughs and shires, with council members elected by a property-based franchise. Queensland has cities, towns and shires and a parliamentary franchise. In South Australia members of the cities, corporate towns and district councils are elected by ratepayers. Western Australia has cities, municipal towns and shires, and Tasmania cities and municipalities; both states use the parliamentary franchise.

Local government bodies are controlled by the state parliament, without any intermediate group equivalent to the British County Council or the local and city councils of the USA. They pass bylaws in relation to such things as roads, sewerage, water and health. The fragmentation of the large cities into so many authorities makes for difficulties: in Sydney there are some forty councils. Only Brisbane has a single controlling council for the whole metropolitan area. New South Wales has a number of bodies called County Councils formed on an *ad hoc* basis to deal with specific fields such as water supply, or in the case of Cumberland County Council with planning of the Sydney region; but it has no teeth for implementation. In other states there are also statutory bodies concerned with particular purposes: roads, water, electricity, even fire fighting, which is of great importance both in the country and in the bush fringed suburbs.

THE PUBLIC SERVICE

The administration of laws passed by one federal and six state governments naturally requires a lot of public servants; seven services in fact, differing in detail. All are controlled by an authority appointed by Cabinet, but varying in name and composition. All are generally built from candidates recruited through examination and organised in grades (85 per cent of US civil servants are recruited by examination). The rights of the public service employee are firmly embodied in statutes, so that he can appeal against wrongful dismissal or promotions which bypass him in seniority. The Commonwealth public service appoints graduates to advanced grades, but in the states only some relaxations for service with the forces exempt applicants from starting in the very junior grades. There is more emphasis on professional specialist qualifications in high administrative posts as against the British tendency to use arts graduates of the older universities, and less recruitment from graduates in general than in the USA. On the other hand, there is a fair sprinkling of old boys from the 'Great Public Schools' (*sic*) in the Department of Foreign Affairs. Australia has a higher proportion of civil servants in relation to population than either Britain or the USA, even allowing for the inclusion in Australian figures of railway staff, teachers and other state employees.

COMMONWEALTH VERSUS THE STATES

The relationship between the Commonwealth and the state parliaments is one that can have phases of acute tension, suspicion and even hostility, almost invariably caused by finance. Since federation, control of the country's finances has come increasingly to be in the hands of the central government. The Commonwealth has the exclusive power to raise money by loan for all seven Australian governments, and in return it assumes responsibility for all state debts and contributes to their interest payments. The amount and the allocation of the moneys is decided by the Loan Council, established in 1928 and consisting of one representative from each state and one from the Commonwealth; usually they are the Premiers and Prime Minister respectively. But the Commonwealth has two votes and the casting vote, although unanimous approval is considered necessary on really vital issues.

The Loan Council meetings are held in Canberra and generally at the same time as the Premiers' Conference, a less formal and non-constitutional body which provides a second forum for debate. For this the Commonwealth provides a secretariat; the Prime Minister takes the chair and has several senior ministers with him. The state Premiers generally have only one supporting minister, but all have their own groups of experts. Not surprisingly, finance tends to dominate the agenda, but other important decisions are also taken: agreement in 1946 on the linking of the rail systems and wartime measures are two examples. The states have formidable safeguards against domination from the centre in their own parliaments which must pass any agreements reached at the Premiers' conferences.

The main subject remains the disbursement to the states of Commonwealth grants, which come from the income tax levied throughout the country. A formula based on area, population and rate of increase is used as a broad measure and gives New South Wales 34 per cent, Victoria 25 per cent, Queensland 15 per cent, Western Australia 10·5 per cent and Tasmania 4·5 per cent. In addition further grants are made to Tasmania and Western Australia (and in 1970–1 to South Australia) as 'claimant states' which are in need of help to sustain living standards compatible with the rest of the country. The Commonwealth also disburses large grants for specific development projects such as railways, irrigation and power projects; these now account for 20 per cent of the total moneys handed over to the states, and are much sought by the Premiers. The

Commonwealth may also finance bounty payments on agricultural products or industrial exports. In February 1972 grants totalling $A90 million (about $US 108 million and £44 million) were made to the states to boost their flagging economies.

The Consolidated Revenue Fund of the Commonwealth receives all the money from income tax (accounting for about 60 per cent of the total), from customs and excise (25 per cent), sales tax and so on. Until 1971 it also received payroll tax, but this is now administered by the states. Money for all government purposes must be appropriated from the Consolidated Fund and so go through the test of parliamentary debate. By its control of income tax the Commonwealth can inject spending power or seek to check inflation.

The citizen fills in a tax return after 4 June each year; on it he states his income from all sources and claims allowance for dependents and for certain expenditures. These include medical costs, costs of prescribed drugs, life insurance premiums on a generous scale and educational costs (including fees for private schooling); they do not include the interest element in house mortgages. Meantime tax based on a coding for salary has been deducted at source and in due course the taxpayer will receive either a demand for more tax, or more often a refund of tax based on his return when duly checked. Exemption for lower incomes and generous treatment of the wealthy leaves the middle income range and especially the man on a fixed income as the chief carrier of the tax burden; recent changes have marginally lightened the load.

While the states may levy tax on incomes they do not find it politic, since the collection of the Commonwealth tax takes precedence. Only 20 per cent of state revenues come from tax: of this 30 per cent is motor taxation, a further 20 per cent land tax, lotteries, stamp duties and so on. Over 40 per cent of state revenues come from Commonwealth payments and a further 20 per cent from their own business undertakings.

The Reserve Bank of Australia, set up by the Commonwealth in 1960, controls credit and note issues and is a powerful central regulator of the economy. It also controls the lending policy of the trading banks by fixing a percentage which they must deposit with the Reserve Bank. The Commonwealth Banking Corporation controls the Commonwealth Trading Bank, the Commonwealth Savings Bank and the Commonwealth Development Bank (created to help with large developmental projects). The trading banks are the cheque issuing, deposit and overdraft banks for the general public and for private industrial concerns; some also run savings banks. The major trading banks are: the Commonwealth Trading Bank of Australia; Australia and New Zealand Banking Group Ltd; Bank of Adelaide; Bank of New South Wales; Commercial Bank of Australia Ltd; the Commercial Banking Company of Sydney Ltd; the National Bank of Australasia Ltd. The general share of the trading banks in the country's financial life is less dominant now, largely because of the growth of hire purchase. Many have sought to share in this growing business by associating with finance companies. The 'never never' system entails about $A2,000 million of outstanding debt each year.

CURRENCY

Australian currency was decimalised in 1966 when the units were changed from pounds, shillings and pence to dollars and cents. There had been much controversy over the names for the new currency. Sir Robert Menzies, then Prime Minister, had wanted to call the new unit a 'royal', but this was widely rejected, not unnaturally perhaps; so were the many other suggestions which included possibilities like 'austral'. But the dollar won the debate and is distinguished from the many other dollars in world currencies by the sign $A. Coins are in values of one, two, five and twenty cents and have delightful designs based on Australian plants or animals. Notes are in values of one, two, five and twenty dollars; the one dollar note has the Queen on it, the others commemorate famous Australians of the past; all are watermarked with a delineation of Captain Cook.

The Australians felt confident enough not to devalue along with sterling in 1967, although this had an adverse effect on some primary export industries. In 1971, it was announced that the Australian dollar would in future be pegged to the US dollar in exchange rates. In October 1972 the Australian dollar was worth 48·45 new pence in sterling and 1·19 US dollars. In December 1971 the Australian dollar was appreciated 6·3 per cent in terms of the US dollar. The floating of sterling in June 1972 meant a devaluation of the pound which caused losses to Australian rural exports.

THE LAW

While stemming from the British legal system, the federal structure has led to important variations in Australian law. A valid Commonwealth law overrides any state law in the same field. Australia, like the USA, shares the British tradition of laws enacted by parliament operating alongside the great body of common law as evolved through the courts. Below the High Court in the pyramid of justice are the subordinate federal courts; but these are few and from 1968 the chief has been the Commonwealth Superior Court. Each state has a Supreme Court and a system of lower courts which vary in name, such as Court of Petty Sessions, Magistrates' Court and so on, with higher courts such as District and County Courts. The lower civil courts are usually presided over by a stipendiary magistrate or a commissioner. In most instances appeal may be made against the magistrates' decision to one of the higher courts and tried by a single judge. Further appeal goes to the Supreme Court of the state, and in certain cases to the High Court of Australia. Ultimate appeal to the Privy Council in London was effectively abolished in 1968, although there is still limited provision for direct appeal from a state Supreme Court to the Privy Council.

There are two types of criminal court: courts of summary justice dealing with minor offences and the higher courts with judge and jury. Appeals go to the Supreme Court and, with leave, to the High Court. The High Court of Australia, with a Chief Justice and six other justices, usually meets in Melbourne, but is held when required in other state capitals. In almost all instances it acts as a court of appeal from the state Supreme Court on matters of serious dispute.

The Commonwealth Parliament can and does vest the state courts with powers to enforce Commonwealth law and to deal in the first instance with disputes arising from it. This structure differs from that of the United States for instance, with its two parallel sets of federal and state courts. Judges and magistrates are appointed by the executive and, increasingly, magistrates are paid officials rather than honorary appointments.

In 1959 the Commonwealth took up its rights under the constitution to legislate in matters of divorce and marriage. Divorce is now effectively available by consent, but there are stringent safeguards for the children. The constitution contains no positive 'bill of rights' for the individual citizen; unlike the US Constitution, there is no specific provision for the protection of fundamental liberties in opinion, speech, association, property, etc, against all governments, although freedom of trade among the states is protected and religious toleration and fair payment for property compulsorily acquired are guaranteed against the Commonwealth. These democratic liberties are protected only through the procedures of the common law tradition. These work well and to the benefit of the citizen in peace time at any rate, but leave both federal and state parliaments in a strong position to curtail them in times of emergency.

There is some anxiety at the growing federal security service, which is not subject to public debate; the problem facing any democracy in reconciling personal liberty with national security faces Australia, with bitter inter-party dispute on the activities of security agents.

There is some ambivalence in the Australian attitude to the law. Generally very law abiding citizens, with a deep respect for the concepts of justice, they have at the same time a suspicion of the machinery of the law, an attitude probably going back to the early days of the six colonies. Autocratic military and police authority was wielded not only in the first convict settlements but in the later turmoil of the gold rush era and the spread of settlement across the land. The bushrangers who flourished in the middle years of the nineteenth century often had a good deal of tacit support if not actual connivance from the public. The myth of Ned Kelly, Irish, rebellious and poor, still has a strong hold on the Australian imagination.

The police are controlled by the individual states and there are no decentralised municipal or county police as in Britain and the USA. Organisation is broadly on the British pattern, from the Commissioner through the District Superintendent (or Regional Superintendent in South Australia) down through Inspectors for Sub Districts and Sergeants or Constables in charge of Stations. The degree to which the police are armed varies with the states, from the almost permanently holstered officer in New South Wales to the unarmed Tasmanian. It has been pointed out that the number of violent attacks on the police increases in proportion with the degree of arming. The public attitude to the police is generally less friendly than in most British communities, though they are as efficient and sympathetic as any in times of crisis like kidnapping. Relationships are perhaps a good deal less strained than between public and police in the USA; as in a number of features, Australia lies somewhere between Britain and America. The courage and patience of the New South Wales police in a recent 'siege' by an unbalanced young man was a model to all.

PARTIES AND POLICIES

The Liberal Party was formed in 1944 in its present form, by Sir Robert Menzies, from the survivors of the older United Australia Party. This in turn derived (1931) from the union of a Nationalist Party with a small dissident Labor group. During the 1930s the United Australia Party was in power and became largely discredited as being far to the right and over dominated by financial interests. It was swept from power by Labor. The present Liberal Party has more in common with the British Conservative Party in its doctrines than with the small British Liberal Party. It favours 'private enterprise' and associated capitalism, contributory schemes for social welfare and government support only for massive development projects unlikely to attract sufficient private capital.

The Country Party, which provides a number of cabinet ministers and the Deputy Prime Minister under the present coalition with the Liberals, has power out of proportion to its size. Electorates are weighted in favour of the rural voter and the mainstay of the party is the smaller farmer. As already

———

Canberra, the national capital. Parliament House (to be replaced by a new building just behind it) is left central across the lake, and the War Memorial is in the foreground.

Sydney from the north. The harbour bridge, Opera House and city centre are in the middle distance.

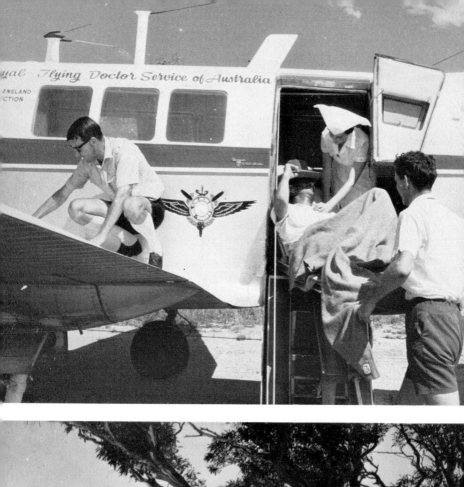

described, it benefits from the voting system, and holds an enviable corner position between Liberal and Labor groups. Sharing many Liberal beliefs, the Country Party also has a special attachment to land ownership, and is concerned with the problems of the primary producer, with collective marketing and with credit facilities. It has a difficult road ahead in these years of rural recession. The party also relies on support of the small country towns, also declining; decentralisation of industry is an important aim.

The Australian Labor Party, or ALP, which developed as the political wing of the trade union movement, grew first in New South Wales. The ALP supports the collective as against the individual approach, believing in the values of the welfare state. The Australian variety of labour politics has been described as 'socialism without doctrine' and the Party has a highly pragmatic approach, a tendency to avoid stressing nationalisation as a dogma. Although there were brief, earlier periods in power, Labor came into its own during and immediately after World War II under two remarkable leaders, Chifley and Curtin. In the wave of reconstruction and planning that followed the war everywhere, Labor brought in much welfare legislation in spite of constitutional stumbling blocks

———

At an isolated cattle property in Queensland an injured stockman is transferred to a Flying Doctor's plane to be taken to hospital. This unique aerial service flies more than 400,000 miles each year to bring expert medical attention to people living at lonely outposts, over an area of about 2,000,000 square miles of the continent.

The Snowy Mountains Hydro Electric Project, started in 1949, is due for completion by 1974. Here a hydrographer makes his way by ski in the course of collecting data. Normally the melted snow and heavy rain of the mountains would run to the sea; now it is being harnessed for power and irrigation by an immense engineering feat.

D

over banking, aviation and a comprehensive national health scheme. In the 1970s it seems that the Liberal/Country Party coalition may have run its course and the Australian elector may be ready to 'give the other chap a go'.

But to win the confidence of enough electors, Labor will have to overcome its bogey of internal strife. The Liberals, too, have their splits, and it was such dissension that led to the 1971 downfall of John Gorton as Prime Minister; but on the whole they have been more successful at papering over the cracks. The ALP has to placate the more militant left wing elements of the Trade Unions. The 'cold war' period of the 1950s saw the Irish Catholic vote split away from the ALP on the grounds that the party was pro-communist. A new party was formed, the Democratic Labor Party or DLP, in 1957. So bitter is the feud that DLP supporters are encouraged to make Liberal or Country Party candidates their second preference when voting. It is not an exaggeration to say that the splitting of the Labor vote has effectively ensured the long reign of the Liberal/Country Party coalition.

The Communist Party, formed in 1920, achieved a maximum membership of some 23,000, which dwindled rapidly after the invasion of Hungary. It, too, has been split internally according to pro-Russian or pro-Chinese thinking. Of the 5,000 or so members now, over half are industrial centres in New South Wales. There is also the expected scatter of left wing intellectuals who are party members. Some have found a new home in the recently formed Australia Party, as yet, like the Communists, unrepresented in parliament, but planning to contest at least forty seats at the next election. Their concern is with the problems of excessive foreign investment in the country, as they see it, with tax reform, education and welfare; they will probably give their preferences to the ALP. A proposed new political party is being launched called the Farm and Town Party. The Australian League of Rights is an extreme right wing group. The widespread 'agin the government' feeling that afflicts every party in power results in a large sprinkling of Independents of varying hue. Party politics are dominant in the Senate and paramount in the states. There have in the past been long periods of Labor rule in New South Wales and Queensland (where they abolished the upper house in 1922) and in Western Australia. While each party has a number of 'safe seats' there is not the long standing domination over large regions found in the USA where historical and regional groupings remain very important.

DEFENCE

The total defence budget accounts for about 3·5 per cent of the gross national product annually. The shares of the three forces are tabulated:

	Personnel 1971		*Expenditure 1970–1*
	Total	*Permanent*	*in $A000*
Navy	22,948	17,820	243,010 (US credit 26,122)
Army	84,260	45,200	413,889 (US credit 11,377)
Air Force	24,398	22,700	312,791 (US credit 39,792)

The estimated total defence budget for 1971–2 is $A1,252, 383,000. The figures for the army include some 16,000 young men conscripted by ballot from their age group at twenty. Conscription has been a source of bitter controversy in Australia: it was rejected at two (non-constitutional) referenda held during World War I, but was applied with little protest in World War II. A full national service scheme operated 1951–9 and the present selective scheme dates from 1965. The ALP is pledged to end it but to retain the current level of defence spending.

There is a Minister for Defence and one for each of the Army, Navy and Air Departments; not surprisingly there is some friction. The Defence Department controls over-all strategy, policy, deployment and expenditure, and co-ordination with other activities like intelligence. The ALP envisages a welding of all the service departments into a Ministry of National

Defence. A Joint Staff College was opened in 1970. The navy has a college at Jervis Bay, an exclave of the Australian Capital Territory on the coast of New South Wales which is also navy headquarters. The air force has its own staff college and the army has the Royal Military College in Canberra, which has university status as a college of the University of New South Wales.

Australians have a well-earned reputation for military skill and daring. The military past and present of the country is passionately cared for in the War Memorial in Canberra. A massive building, it lies at the foot of the wooded slopes of Mount Ainslie at the end of a long clear vista across the lake from Parliament House. Round a Pool of Reflection run galleries of relics, paintings and models of horrific reality of great battles from the Somme to New Guinea, from North Africa to Korea. The Hall of Memory with its high dome, mosaic walls and sculptured warriors echoes to the feet of half a million visitors every year.

EXTERNAL LINKS

Australia's foreign policy in the past has swung from the passionate devotion to the Crown that marked Sir Robert Menzies, to the rather inwards looking stance of the ALP at times. It was a Labor statesman, Dr Evatt, who became President of the United Nations 1948–9. As a founder member of the UN Australia has contributed to peace-keeping forces in Cyprus and the Congo and sent troops to Korea.

A generous foreign aid programme accounting for 0·75 per cent of the gross national product includes a heavy commitment to the Territory of Papua-New Guinea; other contributions go to the Colombo Plan and through international agencies such as the Asian Development Bank. Every year many hundreds of Asian students attend universities in Australia.

The country's increasing orientation towards the Pacific

region and south-east Asia is seen in the system of alliances built up over the last twenty years. ANZUS (1952) involves Australia and New Zealand along with the United States in a mutual security pact. The South East Asia Treaty Organisation (SEATO) was started in 1954 and includes such bizarre bedfellows as New Zealand, Pakistan, Thailand and France along with Britain and the United States. ASPAC (Asian Pacific Council), formed in 1966, is a consultative group of which Australia is a founder member.

The reduction of British forces east of Suez has led to a reappraisal of strategy for Australia. The last combat troops left Vietnam at the end of 1971; but Australian instructors will remain. She also retains commitments for training, personnel and supply in south-east Asian countries such as Thailand, Malaysia and Singapore. Broadly her defence strategy rests on strong maritime defence and an air umbrella based on the 'Phantom'. The controversial F111 swing-wing fighter bombers ordered from the United States will take over. The United States enjoys defence facilities for communications on the west coast and has projects in central desert areas that cause some anxiety by their very secrecy.

Australia maintains High Commissioners in fourteen countries of the British Commonwealth and thirty-nine consular missions overseas in other countries, all of which reciprocate with missions in Australia. She was among the first Commonwealth countries to recognise Bangladesh in early 1972. Although China has become a major customer for Australian wheat the country is not yet recognised diplomatically. This, too, is liable to change, for in 1971 the ALP anticipated President Nixon by sending a delegation to Peking and making recognition of China one of its policies if elected. It also queries the dependence on the USA which has been so firmly part of external relations since the war and the economic dependence on Japan. But these stern realities are nevertheless likely to remain very important to the Australia of the 1970s.

3

How the Country is Made Up

THE states and territories making up the Commonwealth of Australia are very varied in size and population as the table shows. Although power has become increasingly placed in the central government the states retain jealously their individual parliaments and are stern rivals with one another in claiming moneys from the Commonwealth government. They also compete overseas for potential investment and migrants.

State	Area in sq miles	Population 1971	Capital
New South Wales	309,433	4,589,556	Sydney
Victoria	87,884	3,496,161	Melbourne
Queensland	667,000	1,823,362	Brisbane
South Australia	380,070	1,172,774	Adelaide
Western Australia	975,920	1,027,372	Perth
Tasmania	26,215	389,874	Hobart
Territories (Internal)			
Northern Territory	520,280	85,519	Darwin
Australian Capital Territory	939	143,843	Canberra

NEW SOUTH WALES

New South Wales is the oldest, the most populous and the wealthiest state, with a history that began with the first European settlement in 1788. In the early days it covered half the continent but by 1863 the rise of the other colonies had pruned it to its present shape and size, covering a tenth of Australia but containing a third of all Australians. Landscapes vary from humid subtropical banana and sugar fields along the North Coast to the high plateaus of the Snowy Mountains; from a closely settled coastal fringe including industrial conurbations to arid inland plains 700 miles to the west. Between lies a steep fretted belt of forested scarps edging the sheep and wheat country of the Western Slopes, which lead down to the fertile, irrigated farms of the Murray valley.

Industry accounts for 75 per cent of the state's economic output, agriculture for 18 per cent, mining for 6 per cent and forestry for 1 per cent. One in three migrants is destined for New South Wales, and most likely for Sydney, Newcastle or Wollongong. There are quite large and attractive inland towns: Bathurst is the oldest and has been suggested as an inland capital; Orange, Dubbo, Tamworth, Parkes and Goulburn are others with history and pride.

Sydney is the home of one in five Australians and is one of the world's great modern cities. The unique character is caught by an editor of the *Sydney Morning Herald*, J. Douglas Pringle (*Australian Accent*, 1965, p 190):

> It is a gay, pagan, boisterous, raffish city, full of oysters and beer and pretty girls in summer frocks, and white sails in the harbour. But full also of hard faced business men and angry policemen shouting at street corners, and traffic jammed in narrow streets.

The choicest living areas are in the harbour side suburbs like Potts Point or on the North Shore. The business area centres on the site where the first settlers struggled to survive beside the old Tank Stream. High office blocks including the round skyscraper in Australia Square overtop the remaining elements of the regency city. Industrial suburbs stretch south to Botany Bay, now surrounded and polluted by heavy industry, and west along the harbour. To the south-west endless flat suburbia stretches to the hill edge. Along the eastern side are more than twenty fine beaches, and fine parks lie at northern and southern extremities. The almost empty bush of the inland hilly margins laps the outer suburbs.

The Labor Party has always been strong in New South Wales and was in power from 1941 to 1964; the present Liberal/ Country Party coalition has only a slender majority. The outlying parts of the state resent the strongly centralised control from Sydney and there have been active movements towards new states in the far north in New England and in the Riverina. In turn, New South Wales, which might well be big enough to be a viable nation on its own, is most resentful of central control from Canberra.

VICTORIA

Victoria covers only 3 per cent of Australia but has about 30 per cent of the people and is the most closely settled. The area, roughly equal to England and Wales, contains plateaus swelling to 6,000ft through thickly forested foothills; to the north are the slopes of the Murray and to the south the green, temperate lands of Gippsland and the Western District, east and west of Melbourne respectively. Only in the far north-west is there a glimpse of arid Australia. The rest is well watered most years; too well watered for Sydneysiders, who scorn the chill damp winter as much as the tame sandy beaches of Port Phillip.

Two temporary military settlements were tried in 1803 and 1824, but the first permanent settlers came from New South Wales overland and across the Bass Strait from Tasmania in the 1830s. Victoria became a separate colony with responsible government in 1851 just as the gold rushes began that were to treble her population. The diggers stayed to provide labour for industrial growth behind tariff protection, and Victoria remains the most highly industrialised state. She produces a third of the country's vehicles and machinery, and over half the rubber and clothing and a third of the chemicals. The state attracts about as many migrants as New South Wales.

Early Liberal governments established a number of state

enterprises; the Labor Party has had less influence, for the drastic split which formed the DLP (see p 54) was centred in the state and the Country Party is strong in the closely settled rural areas.

Melbourne dominates the state, but there are well established inland centres like the old gold town of Ballarat, Bendigo, and market centres like Shepparton, while Geelong is an industrial port and Westernport a new industrial centre. Melbourne and Sydney are perennial rivals. The built-up area undulates through leafy expensive suburbs to the hill country in the east; to the west it sprawls over level basalt plains. The focal area is the Golden Mile of Collins Street, which is still the financial heart of Australia. Tall blocks have mushroomed since building heights were de-restricted in the 1950s, but central Melbourne retains much Victorian solidity. The new federal parliament sat here from 1901 to 1927 and a few residual functions remain. The reputation for solemnity against Sydney's gaiety is shattered in the horse-racing season and by the winter frenzy of Australian rules football. And Melbourne has a long tradition in the arts and letters.

QUEENSLAND

Queensland is the second largest state after Western Australia; it covers a fifth of the continent and has 14 per cent of the population. Queensland is the 'Sunshine State' and the Queenslander can often be identified by the width of his hat brim, his slower speech and the fact that he chooses the shady side of the street.

Stretching north to within eleven degrees of the Equator, Queensland has landscapes that range from thick tropical jungle to desert sand dunes; from lush green along the eastern margins to the dusty red cattle country of vast interior basins; and from rank tropical grassland round the Gulf of Carpentaria to sombre brown-earthed sheep country and the wheat fields of the Darling Downs.

The state was born as a penal settlement in 1826 for the most intractible of the convicts sent to New South Wales. Later its fine inland pastures brought squatters and then sporadic mineral rushes increased migration. The colony became independent of New South Wales in 1859. More than once the northern parts, a thousand miles from the capital, have threatened secession. Plantations for sugar and bananas were established using islanders brutally collected from the Pacific and working under conditions of near slavery. They were repatriated after federation and the stage set for the 'triumph in the tropics', which is the state's proud boast. Nowhere else in tropical latitudes do white men toil as they do here. There have been many Italian migrants, but only 10 per cent of the total migrants go to Queensland.

Primary production outweighs industry and this has meant relatively slow growth; the government is concerned to attract new industry from other states and overseas. And large coal contracts have been signed with Japan. Because of the size and shape of the state, Brisbane, which lies in the south-east corner, has a less dominant share of the people and prosperity than most other state capitals. Railways run inland from the ports of Cairns, Townsville and Gladstone, tapping the interior. Even so, four out of ten live in Brisbane.

The city lies, encircled by low hills, on the Brisbane River; ships sail past mangrove swamps at the mouth and then 18 miles upstream to wharves in the heart of the city. The core is a close net of streets on the north bank, with Victorian Gothic grandeur that made little concession to the climate. Industrial suburbs lie south of the river and upstream to the Ipswich coalfield. Palm-lined streets climb the slopes in St Lucia and spread along the bayside. The hurried business man from the south relaxes a little in the balmy air of Brisbane. Paradoxically, however, it is in Queensland that the strictest censorship laws are applied. Here, too, the Aborigine has a pretty raw deal; although Queensland took the honour of appointing the first Aboriginal Senator to Canberra in 1971. The Labor Party ruled from 1915 to 1957 and in 1922 abolished the upper house. There has been a lot of state involvement in social and economic affairs, not always successful. But Queensland does have the most comprehensive health service, if (according to some) the worst educational system in Australia.

SOUTH AUSTRALIA

South Australia, fourth in the population league, covers over 9 per cent of the country. All but 1 per cent of her people live in the southern quarter. Here, Yorke and Eyre Peninsulas thrust south into more temperate zones; the stark Flinders Ranges soften south into green rolling landscapes behind Adelaide. The northern two-thirds 'beyond the counties' is a desert of rocky gibber and sand-dunes. There are a few vast sheep stations, the isolated space research installations at Woomera, the opal diggers at Coober Pedy and Andamooka and the new natural gas field of Gidgealpa.

South Australia is a proud state; less generous compatriots describe it as rather smug and snobbish. But even if this were true (and it would be much diluted by migration and industry), it would stem understandably from historical origins. For the colony began as a free settlement in 1834, with no convicts, although the great land experiment was tempered by harsh realities and at times convicts were used. Later the discovery of copper saved the colony, which has iron, but little coal and less water.

The long-lived Liberal Ministry of 1938–65 set about attracting industry and migrants by tax and housing policies; now 60 per cent of output is industrial with a bias towards electrical and consumer goods and vehicles. The state is thus the first to feel any economic draughts which lead to reduced consumer spending. Wheat, barley, wool and 75 per cent of Australian wines come from South Australia. A unique drained swamp-land forms a distinctive region in the south-east corner which has felt isolated enough from the capital to talk of secession in the past. South Australia re-elected a Labor Government in 1970.

Adelaide contains 65 per cent of the population. The centre

retains the grace and beauty of Light's design in 1836. The core area lies south of the green belt along the Torrens, and beyond it industrial suburbs stretch to Port Adelaide, which has to be maintained by dredging. Inland are the low wooded slopes of the Mount Lofty scarp. Intolerable summer heatwaves can sweep Adelaide and people gasp anxiously for a cool change from the Bight.

WESTERN AUSTRALIA

Western Australia, the awakening giant, covers a third of the continent but has only 8 per cent of the people. But the rate of growth 1966–71 was over 21 per cent, more than twice that of any other state. The iron fields of the north-west with six new towns and two old ones that have grown out of recognition account for 10 per cent of the state's urban increase. Even so, 68 per cent of Westralians live within twenty-five miles of the centre of Perth, and 81 per cent in towns. The temperate south-west has the wheat and wool country and the lovely forests of karri and jarrah trees. The inland third lies in desert sands which reach north-west to the coast between the rocky plateaus of the Hamersley and Kimberley regions.

For long the isolation from the wealthy eastern states bred a resentment among the people of Western Australia, so deep that in 1935 they voted by three to one to secede from the Commonwealth; the move was vetoed in London. The people from the east have called them the 'sandgropers' and in return are known as 't'othersiders'. Now Western Australia feels she is emerging as a vitally important part of the whole country.

The colony began with a military settlement at Albany in 1826, established to warn off the French. The final British annexation of Australia was completed by the establishment of a free colony on the Swan River in 1829. But it ran into much greater difficulties than South Australia: the land was poor, there was not enough labour and stagnation blighted the colony for decades. Transportation was introduced and maintained much later than in the east; the gold rushes of the late nineteenth century and the opening of wheat lands then also gave some impetus. Western Australia did not have responsible government until 1890.

Primary products account for over half the output and are increasingly dominated by minerals. The fine city of Perth lies along the banks of the Swan with the core area on the north. Urban freeways lead north-west to the desirable river and seaside suburbs and south across the Narrows Bridge to the more industrialized suburbs. To the east lies an expanse of typical flat Australian suburbia. Fremantle, a growing modern port, is at the river mouth, spreading out from the white limestone buildings put up by convicts a hundred years ago. The Kwinana Freeway sweeps south behind the dunes to a new industrial complex.

Western Australia was the cradle of the Country Party, concerned with the problems of the smaller wheat farmers. The state has also had important periods of Labor then Liberal rule; in 1970 the ALP won a narrow victory.

TASMANIA

Tasmania, the smallest state by far, offers a complete contrast with the gigantic Western Australia. It covers only 1 per cent of the country's total area and has 3 per cent of the people. The western half is an ice-scoured plateau of forests and lakes edged by jagged snow-capped ridges. Fertile land is restricted to a narrow strip along the north coast and to the river valleys. Here, settlement is close, by Australian standards, with smiling landscapes and a weather pattern dominated by westerly depressions; this gives the English image associated with the island. The comparison should be with Scotland, for like that country, Tasmania is a land of emigration. The rate of growth in 1966–71 was only 4·9 per cent, compared with the all Australian figure of 9·7 per cent. Only about one in a hundred migrants goes to Tasmania.

The colony was founded in 1803 and in 1825 became the first to separate from the parent New South Wales; its name was changed from Van Diemen's Land to commemorate Abel Tasman. The early colonial period was one of brutality; the worst convicts were sent to the island's remote settlements, and the Aborigines were virtually exterminated. The Vandiemonians who migrated to the mainland were a rough lot on the whole. The island's own mineral boom came with tin and copper towards the end of the century; the revival of mining is injecting new life today.

The famous apple industry grew with refrigerated shipping and the island produces most of Australia's hops for beer. But her major resource lies in water power, which has attracted smelting and paper industries to use mineral and forest supplies. With dairy products they account for 62 per cent of output.

With some 33 per cent of the island's people Hobart is much the least dominant among state capitals. Another 15 per cent live in Launceston at the northern end of the lower midland corridor. A string of sizeable towns along the north coast facing Victoria is growing. Hobart's site is perhaps the grandest in Australia, between the deep Derwent estuary and the forested slopes of Mt Wellington. The old harbour with its stone ware houses has a charm and character not found elsewhere in Australia. Suburbs climb steeply inland and south along both banks of the estuary; heavy industry lies upstream and beyond are the orchards of the wide Derwent valley with the rough tangle of mountains behind. If Tasmania is parochial in outlook, conservative in politics, it is a parish to enjoy and a priceless asset to a continent with so much drought and desert.

INTERNAL TERRITORIES—NORTHERN TERRITORY

This vast expanse of tropical Australia covers 18 per cent of the country and has only some 85,000 people; but this represents a 15 per cent increase since 1966, accounted for by mineral and port development, tourism and defence establishments. The

Territory stretches from steamy monsoonal jungles in the north to deserts in the south. A chequered history began with a military settlement on the north coast in 1824. For a time the region was part of New South Wales, before becoming literally the 'northern Territory' of South Australia, which tried unsuccessfully to sell this piece of real estate to the Japanese in 1877! In 1911 the Commonwealth took it over for £5 million. Chinese settlers came to the gold fields in the late nineteenth century and their descendants have been an important and respected element in the population. There are some 19,000 Aborigines; they are the mainstay of the cattle industry; a fair number remain on formerly tribal lands in Arnhem Land and in the interior deserts.

Darwin has been transformed from a ramshackle and sleepy outpost to a rapidly growing modern city with some well designed tropical architecture. It is an administrative centre and port. The Territory is administered through a partially elected Legislative Council with an appointed Administrator; the voters send one representative to the centre.

INTERNAL TERRITORIES—AUSTRALIAN CAPITAL TERRITORY

The Australian Capital Territory, or ACT, was carved out of New South Wales in 1908, to provide a site 'not less than 100 miles from Sydney' for the new federal capital. It is rolling plateau country edged on the south-west by the foothills of the Snowy Mountains. Outside Canberra, the ACT comprises rough grazing land with better pastures along the Murrumbidgee and its tributary valleys.

But of course Canberra is predominant and has grown by almost 50 per cent since 1966. Something of the city's character will be outlined in Chapter 4. It is a pleasant city and a lively one in which to live, although winter nights are bitter and summer winds can be torrid. The streets are lined with two million trees, many of them exotic varieties that give spring flourish and autumn foliage of a riotous colour unfamiliar over much of Australian landscapes.

The population includes some 38 per cent of public servants in its workforce; the Australian National University and the Commonwealth Scientific and Industrial Research Organisation account for another 25 per cent. A sizeable diplomatic corps adds colour. But socially the population tends to remain segregated in its own groups. There is some resentment of the paternal attitudes of planners and politicians; the city is administered by the Department of the Interior with an elected Advisory Council only able to voice the local views. The ACT sends one Member to the House of Representatives.

EXTERNAL TERRITORIES

Largely through historical accident, Australia stands with Portugal as one of the major residual colonial powers. While Australia is much more committed to shedding these responsibilities, the fact is important both for internal pre-occupations and for external standing. Christmas Island, a small phosphate producing speck in the Indian Ocean, was inherited from Britain in 1958 and the Cocos (Keeling) group of twenty-seven islands in 1955; here a few hundred people, a third of them European, export copra. The uninhabited Antarctic Heard and Macdonald Islands were transferred from Britain in 1947. And Australia stakes the largest territorial claim in Antarctica in a wedge-shaped Territory of 2·5 million square miles; bases are maintained at Davis, Wilkes and Mawson and on Macquarie Island, and the Territory is administered from the Department of Foreign Affairs. Norfolk Island, some 14 square miles and lying 1,000 miles north-east of Sydney, became a Commonwealth Territory taken over from New South Wales in 1913; it is a pleasant tourist resort but otherwise something of an economic liability.

By far the most important Territory is Papua-New Guinea, covering 2 million square miles in the eastern half of the island of

New Guinea. Mountain ranges reach well over 10,000ft in the central highlands and there are humid coastal plains to north and south. Papua, the south-eastern part, was taken over from Britain in 1906, and Australia was given a League of Nations Mandate over the formerly German northern part in 1920; this was redefined as a United Nations Trust Territory in 1946. Papua-New Guinea is administered jointly and considerable progress has been made towards responsible government. There are locally elected councils and a national House of Assembly of 94 members, of whom 84 are elected. Supreme power still rests with the Australian Administrator and his Executive Council, which includes some of the Ministers. The Territory of Papua-New Guinea costs the Australian taxpayer about $A90 million a year. It employs about 35,000 expatriates either in public service or as settlers engaged in timber, tea, coffee, rubber or minerals. Recent developments include copper mining.

The indigenous people number over two million and are mainly Melanesian in origin, but with an incredible array of language and culture, from stone-age tribes in the interior to sophisticated and cash-oriented cocoa growers in Gazelle Peninsula. Ultimate self rule is the official aim. The official date is now set for December 1973 save in foreign affairs and defence; educational and economic advance have been outstripped by the natural aspirations of the people. Racial tensions are quite sharp, with little interchange; indigenous public servants are paid lower salaries than equivalent Australian expatriates on the logical grounds that Australian rates would be far beyond the means of the future independent country, but it makes for resentment meantime. For Australians at home Papua-New Guinea is something of an enigma. Although it offers some career, research and investment opportunities, they would on the whole be relieved to shed this burden and show little enthusiasm for integrating the Territory as a seventh state, as has occasionally but not very responsibly been suggested.

E

4

How They Live

HOUSING

ALTHOUGH predominantly town dwellers, Australians cling to an ideal of space and freedom in housing, greatly preferring one storey, detached homes. Of the 3·2 million private dwellings, 85 per cent are houses and only 8 per cent are flats. Home ownership is also an important goal, and 80 per cent of dwellings are owned or in process of long-term purchase. In the USA about 62 per cent of houses are owner occupied and in Britain about 50 per cent. In Australia the term 'home' is always used, not 'house', a pleasing inference though sometimes a little bizarre in the hands of estate agents.

The prevailing house style has its origins in the early pioneering days when land was plentiful but builders scarce; a single-storey structure was easier. The earliest settlers built houses of mud and shingle which soon gave way to timber and later brick walling. Today the commonest type of house wall is 'brick veneer', that is, one layer of bricks over a timber frame. But 18 per cent of houses are of wood and a further 8 per cent built of 'fibro', sheets of asbestos that are fireproof and need little maintenance but are rather brittle.

The early roofing material was wood shingles, but by the 1840s corrugated iron was appearing, brought out cheaply from England as ships' ballast. Iron was also used to some extent for walls and can still be found in some rural areas. Like the much more widespread corrugated iron roofing, it is fireproof and cools quickly after a hot day. The iron roof also plays a vital role as a water catchment in rural areas without water supplies, which means most rural areas of Australia. Every house in the country has its set of galvanised water tanks to store the precious liquid. And on sheep stations the shearing shed is often a major catchment leading to storage tanks of 10,000 gallons or more. In the towns the heavy red tiles so widespread today began to replace iron by the end of last century; from the air suburban Australia is a sea of terracotta roof tops.

The interior layout still shows remarkable adherence to past traditions. Again, simplicity was decreed by shortage of skill and materials and a four-room style was common, with a shady verandah making a useful extension for living and sleeping in summer. As the costs of land and development began to curtail the size of blocks of land and of houses, the all round verandah gave way to front verandah only. Terraces of houses were built in what are now the inner suburbs of Sydney and Melbourne, with a single verandah running the length, and intricately ornamented with cast iron tracery; after a period of neglect and decay these are now quite highly prized.

The detached house lost its front veranda when builders began to expand the interior space by adding to one of the front rooms, leaving the other one fronted by the remaining half of the verandah as a sort of porch. This has given rise to the L-shaped interior design, which remains very common, with variations for every income group. The rapid growth of car ownership necessary in the sprawling suburbs brought the addition of a 'car port', which is more common than a garage. Where houses are built on a slope, a garage under the house is very common, often linked to a storage or rumpus room; steps lead up to a terrace and the front door. The old Queensland house has for long had this character, with the main dwelling raised on pillars and the space beneath screened in and used for drying clothes, for storing the boat or as wet weather playing space. It also gives a through current of air and is widely used in new housing in the tropical north.

The housing pattern has led to seemingly endless suburbs: Perth, for instance, covers more ground that Greater London, but has only a twentieth of the people. The outer, landward suburbs of Sydney are flat and a rather depressing sprawl and Melbourne is similar. Servicing building blocks with power, sewerage and water is very expensive; large areas of the state capitals remain unsewered as well as many country towns. Individual septic systems are quite common, but can be a health hazard if maintenance is neglected, especially in closely built urban areas where bedrock is near the surface and drainage therefore superficial. Outbreaks of hepatitis have been traced to such situations. Many more housing areas are still dependent on the old 'thunderbox' down the yard, and on the councils for the collection of night soil. To the incomer it all seems anomalous, going as it does with a car in the drive and a refrigerator and television in the house. Electricity is ubiquitous, being more cheaply laid on than water or drains by means of the great loops and tangles of overhead wires and forests of poles that are such a feature of Australian townscapes.

Homes vary in size from quite modest, state built houses of 400–500 sq ft of floor space (four to five 'squares' in Australian usage) to mansions of sixty squares or more. The average suburban bungalow has about twelve squares and a garage or car port. Just over a third of houses have five rooms; a quarter are larger and the rest smaller. The surrounding garden, which with even a tiny patch of lawn will have a rotary power mower, relies on artificial watering. Nowadays a fixed reticulated sprinkler system is quite a status symbol. In addition to the traditional imported species of English garden flowers, there is often a wealth of native Australian blooms, especially flowering shrubs.

A shower is more essential than a bath as a fixture, and there is usually a separate laundry. In the country wood-fired stoves are still quite common; the native hardwoods burn very well in slow combustion stoves. A cheerful open wood fire is often retained even when heating systems are installed. These are desirable in the winter months in the more southerly coastal cities like Melbourne or Hobart and in most inland cities. Oil-fired heaters are increasingly common, often just one large and centrally placed convection heater is used; ducted warm air networks are commoner than hot water radiators. Natural gas is available in a number of centres now. Electricity, though expensive, is also used for under-floor or over-head heating in a few areas. Air conditioning for the summer months is less widespread in homes than offices, though one room may be equipped. The new mining townships of the north have widespread air conditioning.

State houses are available for rent but the waiting list can be three years or more. There is a great scarcity of privately rented property. The radio commercials for one of the major real estate companies begins 'Most Australians wish to own their own homes . . .' and this is indeed true. The occupier of a state-built house has the chance of a very favourable government loan, repayable in up to forty years or even forty-five, transferable to another purchaser and at a low interest rate of 5-6 per cent. House buying in the private sector is more costly. A first mortgage may supply up to $A15,000 depending on the buyer's circumstances, and this will be at 6-7 per cent interest. (See p 10 for sterling and US dollar conversion.) Beyond that, however, a second mortgage will be needed and this can cost as much as 13 per cent in interest. There are fewer building societies than in Britain and borrowing is more often from insurance companies, finance companies or the banks. Some employers will guarantee mortgages for their employees, so keeping the whole interest payment down to the lower rate. But there is no allowance of interest on house loans as a tax deductable expense as there is in Britain, although rates may be allowable; nor is there any equivalent of the US Federal Housing Administration, with its mortgage insurance scheme. Since 1945 the Commonwealth has made long-term loans to the states, to building societies and insurance companies for housing. Saving for home ownership is encouraged by a grant of one dollar for every three a young couple saves, up to a maximum grant of $A500. Ex-service men have a high priority and generous grants for homes.

The cost of housing is high, especially in the metropolitan

centres where a very ordinary block in an uninviting suburb may cost up to $A8,000 before building is even started. This represents a 66: 1 ratio of land cost to the earnings say of a skilled draftsman of on $A90 a week. In 1945 the ratio for similar workers in Sydney was 12: 1. The average house price over the country is $A20,000; this covers a very wide range from the $A8,000 asked for a modest government built 'cottage' to $A500,000 for the fantasy dwellings of Sydney's harbour side. State-built homes account for 15 per cent of the annual building output (under 3 per cent in the USA); the proportion is greater in the Australian Capital Territory (40 per cent), Northern Territory (75 per cent) and South Australia and Western Australia (20–30 per cent).

These houses vary in finish and in facilities. In Canberra they are of a very high standard, but in parts of Western Australia, for instance, very minimal. On the whole, however, Australian homes come complete with cooker and water heater and are generously supplied with built-in cupboards. It is very common in the purchase of a second-hand home to buy curtains and carpets too.

The commonest house type remains the bungalow already described. But among the variations in better off suburbs are modern versions of the 'colonial Georgian' architecture of the squatters: long, low and white with a hipped roof continuing over the veranda. In Tasmania there are more stone houses, dating often from the days of free labour by the convicts; parts of rural South Australia have attractive stone houses. Early this century Spanish influences brought the 'Spanish Mission' theme with its cloisters so well suited to Mediterranean summers. The inter war period saw flourishes of pseudo-Tudor added to the familiar bungalow along with leaded windows and even turrets; during this period suburbs were spreading along expanding commuter rail nets. And in the 1970s the contemporary international idiom with single pitched roofs and quantities of picture windows is being adopted, even though the midday sun has then to be excluded by ugly awnings and blinds.

URBAN LANDSCAPES

The modern office blocks seen in the capitals could be in any city; here too excessive glass has a gross overheating effect counteracted by air conditioning, blinds and other devices. Windows in suburban and rural areas are fitted, like the doors, with fly screens; unsightly but necessary additions.

Public architecture dating from the Victorian era retains the solid confidence of its age. Even in the country towns there will be a handsome town hall with ornate design; in the ghost town of Coolgardie the wide main street still stands, flanked by town hall, post office and bank in lovely pink sandstone, while the houses have almost all gone. The only other two storey building in small townships will be the public house. Films of the past like *Robbery Under Arms* or *The Sundowners* can still be shot on location using existing buildings. In 1969 the latest *Ned Kelly* was made largely in a small town not fifty miles from Canberra: the bitumen road of course was disguised in dust and the television aerials removed.

But the traditional Australian hotel, with verandas running round both floors, supported by thin wooden posts and echoing to the roar of the beer drinkers within, is slowly giving way to the modern motel. Chains of these follow the tourist tracks and have standards that put many British hostelries to shame. The spirit of self service is well suited to the country.

Australians love to own a 'weekender', preferably on the coast. And while they may no longer get away with a shack as in the past, standards are very varied, and again the problem of sewerage arises. An unfortunate ribbon of 'holiday home-scapes' is threatening the coastline from Adelaide to Cairns. Whole new estates are put up by speculative builders, where-ever they can get access to a beach or estuary. There are only minimal planning restrictions. Indeed town planning controls in most states are loose. There are two new 'planned' cities, Elizabeth in South Australia and Canberra the national capital.

In 1911 an international competition for a plan for the new federal capital was won by an American architect, Walter Burley Griffin. Much of his concept has been retained as the city grew, first slowly, then very rapidly from the 1950s. The artificial lake he envisaged was created in the 1960s, and the pattern of wide boulevards and long vistas, crescents and avenues makes Canberra very different from other Australian cities. The low wooded hills rising like dark green islands above suburbia break up the city sprawl, though most are now sacrificed to lookouts, restaurants or television and aircraft warning installations. Canberra is much admired and visited by Australians but not greatly loved. Even though it has stopped absorbing their taxes to any extent, it is probably too aseptic, too tidy, too ordered to appeal to most of them.

The old port-capitals in which 85 per cent of Australians live may have started with ambitious plans, but the exigencies of early colonial life soon modified them. Melbourne and Perth with flat central areas have preserved a rectangular pattern in the city core. Adelaide, planned by William Light, has kept his two foci separated by a green belt along the Torrens River. But Sydney on its harbour-side peninsula and Brisbane and Hobart on their hilly sites have much less of a central grid pattern. Congestion has increased in all the capitals and redevelopment is being forced on them. All have plans and planners, but only Perth gives them statutory authority and only in Brisbane do they benefit from serving a single local government unit. Sydney's ambitious post-war plan was defeated by sheer pressure of housing and industrial needs, and not a little by opportunism. The present plan envisaging 5 million citizens by AD 2000 seeks to develop the city in five individual districts. Water will have to come from far beyond the plateau edge. Melbourne, forecasting a population of $4\frac{1}{2}$ million, expects to cover 2,000 square miles and to develop along seven corridors separated by green wedges. On the whole, plans are more in the nature of realistic hopes for containment than visionary schemes; and there are many who plead for increased attention to decentralisation of people and industry.

LIVING STANDARDS

The Australian standard of living is one of the highest in the world when measured by wages, food consumption, car or television ownership, or power consumption per head. The average weekly wage per male adult employed in December 1970 was $A86.10 (including overtime). The minimum wage laid down by the Arbitration Commission (see page 101) in 1972 was $A51. Just over a third of the total private expenditure is on cars, and just under a third on food; about a tenth goes on drink.

One-fifth of the money spent on food is for meat; only New Zealand has a higher consumption of animal products per head. In 1968, the pounds per head of meat eaten were: New Zealand 222; Argentine and Australia 211; USA 182; Britain 137; and Japan 20. The money spent on cars heads the list; with one car to three people Australia is the world's third most motorised nation after the USA and Canada. Petrol and tyres are cheaper than in Europe and the USA, but the great distances and rough roads make for high running costs. The high food intake and lack of exercise add up to a measure of overeating by the middle class sedentary worker, who in middle life is prone to develop a paunch, or at least a very sleek and well fed appearance. The average calorie intake per day in 1968 was 3,210 (in Britain the figure was 3,160, in the USA 3,100 and Italy 2,860).

Although the European migrants have brought some variety and Greeks and Italians make a good living in the catering industry, the Australian diet is conservative. A fairly heavy breakfast is common, even if not necessarily the traditional steak and two eggs. The ritual of morning tea at eleven or earlier is often accompanied by sweet biscuits or cakes. The midday meal is dinner and includes meat and vegetables and a pudding, while afternoon tea offers more that is sweet. The main evening meal at about 6pm is called tea. Meat or some other protein dish will be followed by a dessert and lots of tea to drink. There are of course many regional and social variations:

lunch and dinner replace dinner and tea in higher social groups. The availability of tropical fruits in the north and abundant peaches and apricots farther south allows for bottling and preserving. Mutton is fairly ubiquitous and is often sold a 'side' at a time for deep freeze storage. Beef tends to need more cooking than prime British beef. Frozen broiler fowls, cheap but tasteless, are sold everywhere. Fruit is surprisingly dear because of the complexities of marketing, but costs can be cut by buying from trucks that drive direct from the growing districts.

Drinking habits are changing slowly too, from the traditional devotion to beer and contempt for 'plonk' (fortified table wines) to the wider consumption of ordinary table wines. Some are very fine indeed, and not expensive; but few escape to overseas markets so the low opinion of Australian wine held abroad is not a true reflection. Wines are often blended from the different growing areas and are available in flagons. The former licensing laws which closed bars at 6pm have disappeared, putting an end to the old 'six o'clock swill' by the working man on his way home.

The Australian housewife is very efficient and has to work very hard in a country with domestic help available only to the wealthy. She cooks and cleans in temperatures that wilt the newcomer, but it takes a toll in the varicosed legs common even in quite young women. They dress smartly rather than with great good taste, are groomed and confident and on the whole much more talkative than their menfolk. In the older cities, notably Adelaide, many still go shopping dressed quite formally with hats and gloves. And the socialite gatherings devoted to fund raising give an airing ground for fashion and gossip. The old time lag in fashion as in everything that resulted from Australia's isolation is vanishing with the jet age, and whether mini, midi or maxi, current western skirt lengths are soon seen on the Australian streets.

The men tend to dress less formally even when accompanying well turned out partners. Shorts are generally permitted for office wear in the summer. Casual summer footwear is the floppy 'thongs', rubber sandals imported in thousands from

Taiwan and Hong Kong. But for men and boys the more en-
closed British sandal is despised as effeminate.

SOCIAL WELFARE

There are two elements in the Australian approach to social
welfare; those benefits which are universal and those which are
available when deemed necessary by a means test. The net
result is a fairly good provision for the less fortunate in a country
blessed, for the present at least, with a low unemployment rate
and high wage rates. But recent surveys have uncovered surprising numbers of people living in poverty; an estimate, for
instance, of 7 per cent in Melbourne. The majority of these are
pensioners living alone and women left as sole breadwinners,
with families to keep.

Universal provision includes a maternity allowance which
increases from $A30 for the first child to $A35 if there are three
or more children under sixteen. It allows for an advance payment of $A20 four weeks before the birth is due. Child endow-
ment (family allowance) is paid to all mothers or guardians of
children up to the age of sixteen (twenty-one for those in full-
time education). The rate is 50 cents per week for the eldest
child, $A1.00 for the second, $A1.50 for the third and then increasing by 25 cents. The Commonwealth contributes to the
costs of medical care by paying for most of the medical costs of
invalid pensioners, age and widow pensioners; it also pays a
basic rate towards the hospital and medical costs of every
patient. It pays prescription charges in excess of over 50 cents.
Any medical costs not otherwise recouped are a tax deductable
expense so that the tax payer benefits.

Cash benefits based on a means test are available for the
aged, widows, chronic invalids, the sick and the unemployed.
The age pensions become available for men at 65 and women
at 60, if they have lived ten consecutive years in Australia (not
necessarily immediately prior to retirement). The maximum
standard rate for a single pensioner was (1972) $A16.50 per

week and for a married couple, $A28.50. The means test is based on both income and property but does not include a house, personal possessions or life insurance with a surrender up to $A1,500. The budget of August 1972 announced that the means test for age pensions would be abolished within three years. The 'means as assessed' allowed to a married couple before they lose all entitlement to a pension is $A52.00 per week, but of course below this figure the pension is geared to the means. Similar criteria are applied to invalid pensions.

The payment of age and invalid pensions accounts for half the expenditure of the National Welfare Fund. This was set up in 1943 and is supplied from the Consolidated Revenue Fund of the Commonwealth (and in turn largely fed from income tax). So in a sense the better off through their tax payments are helping the aged and the sick and the family. Another quarter of the National Welfare Fund goes on Commonwealth contributions to health benefits and an eighth on child endowment. Unemployment and sickness benefits are available to people who have been resident in Australia for twelve months, or who can satisfy authority that they are likely to become permanent residents. Qualifications are fairly stringent and benefits relatively low: a maximum (since February 1972) of $A17.00 per week for a man (along with grants for rural unemployment) with a further $A7.00 if married and $A2.50 for the first and $A3.50 for each subsequent child. During 1969–70, 109,383 people received unemployment benefits and 66,766 sickness benefits. The remaining expenditure from the Fund supplies home savings grants, funeral benefits and the rehabilitation of sick and injured people.

Health benefits are organised on a voluntary contributary scheme through about a hundred non-profit making but competing Funds and Societies which offer benefits related to contributions. The patient normally pays his own costs and then recoups a proportion according to his table of contributions. Refunds range from $A1.60 to $A2.40 for a visit to the doctor's surgery to about $A180.00 for certain operations, in return for quite a modest weekly payment. But it can leave a very big gap when major operations are necessary, or prolonged illness leads to costly treatment. And even the modest contribution is beyond the lowest incomes, leaving some with no health cover from this source.

The voluntary schemes also meet hospital costs on a similar basis; for weekly payments up to $A1.30 benefits up to $A123.00 are available. From 1970 free medical and hospital costs up to the highest offered on the tables were available to those with weekly incomes below $A39.00 and to the sick, the unemployed and new migrants for two months after arrival. About 75 per cent of the population is covered by voluntary health schemes; it is common for membership to be made a condition of employment. Dental care is available on a limited scale for children up to thirteen. Some health funds also offer dental and optical services of their own, for which the patient pays perhaps 60 per cent. Private optical and dental treatment is expensive. Reciprocal agreements waive residential qualifications for citizens of New Zealand or Britain; but with all its faults the British National Health Service gives the Australian in Britain a better bargain than the Briton receives in Australia, especially if he strikes really bad medical trouble. On the other hand the Australian system permits the individual to go direct to the specialist of his choice without going through a general practitioner; not all specialists are highly qualified.

The state play an important role in the social welfare pattern. Their activities lie more in the field of direct service than in cash payments. Welfare foods, flood and fire relief, which are important in a continent of extremes, and public health are among the concerns of the states. They also run probationary services, psychiatric services and some aspects of Aboriginal welfare. Municipal authorities have a limited role: some home help provision is available, but for the most part their contribution is restricted to recreational and cultural aspects of the citizens' wellbeing.

States also help the voluntary welfare services, which play a tremendously important role in Australian life, as would be expected in a nation that esteems self help. The success of many such services and the moneys which invariably follow any appeal on behalf of individuals or groups in trouble are a measure of the generous character of the Australian people. Whether it is right or in keeping with human dignity that the individual should be dependent on publicity and charity is another matter; it is not a thought that seems to occur to many. And there is the real practical weakness that the charity will be distributed unevenly and some will escape the net. The existence of hundreds of autonomous bodies doing good works leads to problems of co-ordination and liaison; but this is being rectified by a growing number of nationwide organisations, for example the National Old People's Welfare Council. There is also co-ordination at state level: New South Wales has a Council for Social Services to which no fewer than 132 organisations concerned with personal welfare are affiliated, ranging from hospital auxiliaries to societies concerned with spastics, epileptics and the mentally handicapped. Many churches undertake welfare work, but in recent years their activities in the field of Aboriginal missions have been gradually lessened. General service organisations like Rotary or Apex are also very active.

Inevitably most welfare activities are concentrated in the cities, but the problems of a vast and thinly peopled interior have also been tackled with courage and imagination. The famous Royal Flying Doctor Service originated in 1928 from the Australian Inland Mission and was inspired by John Flynn, whose ideal was to spread 'a mantle of safety' over the outback. There are seven centres from which planes travel upwards of $1\frac{1}{2}$ million miles a year carrying over 4,000 patients. It is financed from private donations with Commonwealth contributions, with a levy on station owners and a system of fixed charges. The commonwealth runs a separate aerial medical service in Northern Territory.

The general record of public health in Australia is very good, owing much to space and sunshine and generally good diets with plenty of protein. There are no population concentrations of the Asian or even west European dimensions to act as reservoirs of disease, and stringent quarantine regulations have prevented Asian diseases like cholera or plague from becoming serious health problems. There are four isolation hospitals for leprosy: three of them in the tropical north, though the total number of patients is small. Tuberculosis and poliomyelitis are the subject of intensive and successful campaigns of detection and cure as well as prevention. All children under thirteen have free milk at school.

The average Australian can expect to live to 68 if a male and 74 if a female. These figures are very similar to those of Western Europe and North America. The risks of early death are heaviest among young men of 20–4 through motor accidents. And there is a growing and appalling number mutilated or handicapped for life. Australia comes second after West Germany in the world league for accidents. The worst are on long roads that sweep across country, tempting excessive speed because they are deceptively straight, but in reality containing hazards in slight dips or bends and in uneven surfaces. The aggressive streak in the Australian make up must also take some of the responsibility.

Of the killing diseases, heart troubles take the heaviest toll with thromboses and cancers next. In the sunny climate bronchial and lung diseases are less prevalent than in Europe and some parts of the USA. Pneumonia and infant mortality are highest in rural areas and far above the national average among the Aborigines. Drug addiction and venereal disease are causing increasing concern, as in all western nations.

But for the young and healthy at least Australia can be a very good place to live in terms of physical wellbeing. And there is a reasonably good safety net for the less fortunate; a good many fall through the net, but this can happen, too, in more comprehensive schemes. Many Australians, while proud of their philosophy of independence, are far from complacent about the rather patchy nature of their welfare services and feel that the 7–8 per cent of the gross national product (compared with 12–15 per cent in New Zealand and a number of European countries) is perhaps not enough to spend on helping the less lucky inhabitants of their undoubtedly lucky country.

5

How They Work

THE biggest single employer in Australia is the Postmaster-General, with well over 100,000 workers under his control. This is perhaps a rather startling reminder that, in common with other developed, industrialised and urbanised nations, a bigger proportion of the workforce is employed in the 'tertiary' industries, those which serve the community, than in primary industries of farming or mining, or the secondary manufacturing industries. Of a total workforce in 1970 of 5·4 millions, two-thirds worked in offices, shops, administration or the professions and other service activities like garages. Just under a quarter were factory workers and only one in ten worked on the land. Most important of all, only 1·3 per cent were unemployed.

In remote parts there are still some nomadic tribes, but most Aborigines, like the one in the right photograph, work as stockmen on cattle properties or live in settlements or mission stations.

Periodically they set off on a 'walkabout', when for a time they revert to old tribal customs and practise their skills in tracking and hunting game. The left photograph shows Aborigines of the Kimberley region in tropical Western Australia on one of these hunting expeditions, armed with spear and throwing-sticks.

The Australian economy is a mixture of private and public undertakings, all of varying degree of enterprise. The public sector includes all the utilities like water, electricity, roads and railways; the private sector controls the bulk of productive industry. Private and public enterprises compete in the fields of civil aviation, banking, broadcasting and shipping. Government intervention in the private sector is confined entirely to the indirect influence exerted through its monetary and fiscal policies, and through wage policies; but these influences are considerable. While there is total rejection by the Liberal-Country Party coalition of any central economic planning, a future Labor Government might edge towards more direction of the private sector. It is extremely unlikely, however, to alter materially the basic division between public and private ownership, which is widely accepted by the Australian people.

INDUSTRY

Industrialisation was well developed before federation in New South Wales and Victoria and has been continuously encouraged by the Commonwealth. Beginning with the textile

———

Australian Iron and Steel Company works at Port Kembla, New South Wales. The beaches are an invaluable lung.

The main artery of the Northern Territory, the Stuart Highway, links Darwin, the capital, with Alice Springs, almost 1,000 miles to the south. Along it travel trucks, tourist coaches, private cars and the big road trains (like the one shown) which move cattle, petrol, food and equipment up and down the highway. Big trucks drag the road trains of up to four waggons, each about 42 feet long.

F

and other light industries, there has been very rapid growth since the war in the heavy steel, engineering and chemical fields. Technology in Australian industry has very largely been derived from that of more industrialised countries; this tendency has been strengthened by the important role played by foreign capital and by foreign based companies in the industrial field, for they bring with them their own technologies.

Of the 1·4 millions employed in manufacturing industries in 1970, 45 per cent were in New South Wales and 34 per cent in Victoria, leaving only 21 per cent for the rest of the country. In all states except Queensland and Tasmania, 70 per cent or more of the industrial workforce were in the state capital. The largest single group (45 per cent) works in industrial metals, machines and vehicle manufacture, with a further 11 per cent in food, drink and tobacco, 9 per cent in clothing, 6 per cent in textiles and 5 per cent in paper, stationery and printing. Chemicals, bricks, pottery, glass and rubber shared the rest in that order.

THE POWER BASE

Australia lies fifth in the world in her consumption of electricity per head of the population; the first four are Norway, Canada, United States and Britain. The demand in Australia is doubling each decade. The power bases for electricity are plentiful: rich coalfields, two areas suitable for hydro electricity, four known gas fields and at present enough crude oil to satisfy 70 per cent of her needs.

Coal production has shown considerable growth from 20 million tons in 1947 to 47·5 million tons in 1970. Of this, 17·7 million tons were exported, over 16 million of them to Japan. New South Wales produces three-quarters of the country's black coal, exporting about a third of her output. Thick coal seams lie in a vast saucer which is at its deepest far below Sydney; they come near the surface to the north in the Hunter valley and to the south along the Illawarra coast; the western rim approaches the surface round Lithgow. The southerly field provides high quality coal for the coke ovens, thence the blast furnaces of Port Kembla, and is mined from horizontal shafts into the forested mountain slope a few miles inland; the coal trucks run by gravity down to the industrial complex. Mechanisation is also very advanced along the Hunter valley; here, too, the mines seem to lie amid the bush and the miners travel to them from the towns. New port facilities south of Newcastle serve the export trade, but the coal also feeds major local heavy industries. Vast new open cut coal fields are being developed in central Queensland; some of the world's biggest draglines tear out the overburden to expose thick and level seams in the Dawson valley. A new railway has been built to Gladstone and another is under way to a new port south of Mackay. Queensland exports well over half of her output and development is largely by Japanese and American capital. Older, conventional coal mines feed the industries of the Brisbane area in the south of the state. Victoria mines no black coal but has rich deposits of brown coal or lignite in the Latrobe valley, 100 miles east of Melbourne. Open cut workings here feed conveyor belts running direct to a power station. South Australia has more limited lignites at Leigh Creek on the desert margins, with a possible life little more than a further decade. Western Australia has only poor quality black coal round Collie, 100 miles southeast from Perth. Tasmania has very minor fields in the northeast now declining.

Tasmania, however, leads the field in hydro electricity. High mountains in the west are lashed by storms; her central plateau is spattered with lakes that have formed natural reservoirs. When the current Gordon River Scheme in the southwest is complete, the full potential of Tasmanian hydro electricity will have been realised. But the Gordon alone will equal the total output of the Snowy Mountains Scheme on the mainland.

The rivers of the south-east highlands of Australia flow in fairly short courses to the Pacific. The idea of somehow diverting them to water the arid inland had been raised as early as the 1870s. But it was not until 1949 that a Commonwealth Act of Parliament set up the Snowy Mountains Authority to realise this dream. Between then and 1970 some $A800 million have been spent, 17 dams built, 100 miles of tunnels dug and 80 miles of aqueduct put up; 9 power stations can produce 4 million kW, which feed both the New South Wales and Victorian grid systems at times of peak demand. Irrigation water is supplied along the Murrumbidgee and Murray valleys. And the new roads bring in many thousands of visitors to see the installations, to ski in winter, to camp, fish or walk in summer. In the High Country of Victoria there are further smaller hydro electric projects, and several in the wet highlands of north-east Queensland.

Over 75 per cent of the country's electric power comes from thermal stations, half of it from those in New South Wales on or near the coalfields. The first nuclear reactor is planned for Jervis Bay.

Oil and natural gas have been discovered in large quantities under the shallow Bass Strait between Victoria and Tasmania. The oil is piped to the Victorian coast for refining, and the gas now serves Melbourne by pipeline. The first oil and gas field developed is in southern Queensland; from it gas is piped to Brisbane. The central Australian fields are in barren desert country and a gas pipe line over 500 miles long runs to Adelaide. Oil and gas have been found in the Palm Valley region south of Alice Springs. In Western Australia the offshore Barrow Island wells at present provide 7 per cent of Australian oil; gas is being piped to Perth from a field 150 miles to the north of the capital. Exploration continues on a vast scale both on the mainland, but more especially in the offshore basins. Tax concessions help with the huge expenditures involved; even the private citizen can claim oil investments as a tax deductable expense. Drilling has been suspended near the Great Barrier Reef and in the Gulf of Papua pending an investigation into the pollution hazards. Natural gas is expected to provide 10 per cent of primary energy consumption by 1975, and about 70 per cent of crude oil will be home produced in 1972. This proportion will not be maintained with growing demand unless major new fields are developed.

Iron and steel are the sinews of a nation. Although Australia lies only fourteenth in the world league as a steel producer, with 6·3 million tons or 1 per cent of world output in 1967–8, she lies sixth in per capita steel consumption, an important yardstick of industrial development. Almost two-thirds are manufactured at Port Kembla in New South Wales. One-third is made at Newcastle where the first Australian steel was produced in 1915 and which has the country's main shipyard. The dominant firm in Australian industry, BHP, has a near monopoly of steel production. The initials stand for Broken Hill Proprietary Company Limited, but today only the name links it with the mining town of Broken Hill. BHP employs over 45,000 people and has 15 subsidiaries; its interests include coal and iron mining, limestone, nickel and manganese, shipbuilding, wire making, tubes, chemicals and fertilisers; and it has its own cargo fleet. A third much smaller iron and steel works and shipyard are owned by BHP at Whyalla in South Australia. The iron ore of the Middleback Ranges, which was the first to be developed, is smelted using coal brought by ship from New South Wales. The coal ships return to Newcastle and Port Kembla with South Australian iron. BHP also transports its iron from the small islands of iron ore in the far north-west of the continent, Cockatoo and Koolan.

South Australia made the setting up of an iron and steel industry in the state a condition of giving the iron ore leases to BHP. Similarly, Western Australia has obtained the promise of a fully integrated plant in time as part of her negotiations for the sale of her vast resources of iron. So far, blast furnaces have been set up at Kwinana, and a rolling mill using steel brought from New South Wales. At Westernport in Victoria, an integrated iron and steel plant is under construction, jointly owned by BHP and the British firm of Guest, Keen and Nettlefold, which controls the big Lysaght rolling works at Port Kembla. An American company is to set up a steel plant at Jervis Bay.

Until 1959 there was a government embargo on the export of iron ore, because the anxiety felt about future reserves was acute. Great new discoveries in Western Australia were made in the next decade which could well make the country the world's biggest producer by the 1980s. With 51 million tons produced in 1971 she lay fourth; output for 1975 is estimated at 100 million tons. By 1980 iron ore alone could bring in 800 million dollars a year. Over 90 per cent will come from the massive 'mountains of ore' that lie in the harsh Pilbara region of the north-west shoulder of Western Australia. There are three main fields: Mt Goldsworthy, Mt Newman and Mt Tom Price (which has a further new development to the south-west). These are all rich haematite ores. Along the Robe River valley on the western flanks of the plateau are the 'rivers of ore' in the form of thick deposits of limonites. New ports and railways have been built or are planned: Port Lambert, Port Hedland and Dampier are growing as fast as the inland mining towns they are tied to by the iron links of the new railways. Farther south ore is also mined at Kalanooka and exported from the old port of Geraldton, and at Koolyanobbing on the new standard gauge railway to Perth. In Tasmania, the iron mines of the Savage River region are in such wild country that the ore is mixed to a slurry with the plentiful water and piped to the north coast at Port Latta where it is pelletised for export. Two new fields are being developed in the Northern Territory and the iron ore sent out from Darwin. By far the major customer is Japan, although ore is also finding its way in considerable quantities to European markets.

OTHER RAW MATERIALS

Aluminium makes the third of the 'big three' with coal and iron; by 1980 this ore could be earning as much as iron. When the first smelter was set up at Bell Bay in Tasmania after the war, there were no significant known reserves of bauxite in Australia. Since then major fields have been discovered in the far north and west. From Weipa on the western side of Cape York, Comalco, a joint Australian American company, exports alumina overseas and also to feed its own plant at Gladstone, which by 1973 will be the largest in the world. A Swiss Australian consortium, Nabalco, mines leases in the Aboriginal reserve in eastern Arnhem Land where a plant and township at Nhulunbuy are springing up round the dying stump of a tree sacred to the old tribes; saved from the bulldozers as a concession to local feeling, it is withering in the polluting fumes of progress. The Amax company of America will mine ores in the remote Mitchell Plateau in the Kimberley region of the far north-west, as well as in the Darling Range south-west of Perth, which will supply a plant at Bunbury. Also in this region Alcoa, an American company group, obtains ores for its plant at Kwinana. The alumina is sent to the company's smelter at Geelong in Victoria. There is a third smelter at Kurri Kurri near Newcastle.

Lead was third in export value among the minerals in 1970, but was not expected to retain this position. Lead miners receive a valuable 'lead bonus' on top of their wages. Just under two-thirds are mined at Broken Hill and refined at Newcastle and at Port Pirie in South Australia. Most of the rest comes, along with zinc and copper, from the huge mining complex of Mt Isa in the north of interior Queensland and there is a smaller output from Tasmania and from Cobar in New South Wales.

Copper exports are likely to double to be worth $A150 million by 1975 unless the present minor recession deepens. Output is dominated by Mt Isa, which produces 70 per cent; it is railed to Townsville for refining and export. The rest is mined in the great open cut 'Glory Hole' of Mt Morgan in eastern Queensland, at Mt Lyell in Tasmania and Tennant Creek in Northern Territory. Copper is also refined at Port Kembla.

Uranium reserves are enough to supply the export demand;

after a period in mothballs, the model tropical township of Mary Kathleen east of Mt Isa is likely to open up again; Australia expects to be in major uranium production in 1977. There are further deposits in Northern Territory and in the Flinders Ranges of South Australia. Gold, which for so long was Australia's major mineral export, has faded into the shadows of the new ore mountains. Kalgoorlie still gets gold from the famous 'Golden Mile', though mines are closing there and at Norseman farther west; the other gold town is Tennant Creek.

The new wonder mineral of Australia is nickel, as vital to the steel industry as salt to food. Nickel is now known to lie in vast reserves across a shield-shaped area of the ancient rocks of south-west Australia, but figures of reserves and output are hard to find. The Western Mining Company operating at Kambalda now produces some 30,000 tons of nickel a year and is the third largest producer in the non Communist world, which has a total output of some 450,000 tons. The five nickel mines now operating will use the new refinery at Kalgoorlie, reviving after the decrease in gold mining, with the new nickel boom. The notorious Poseidon deposits which marked the high water level in the 1960s mining boom are to be in production in 1972 at Mt Windarra in the arid eastern interior of the state. There are oxide nickel deposits in north-east Queensland, and the search goes on for more bonanzas. Meanwhile, the very beaches of Australia are contributing minerals: rutile from the beach sands of southern Queensland and northern New South Wales and ilmenite from the curving bays of south-west Western Australia. These heavy mineral sands are expected to be worth $A66 million a year by 1975.

MINING AND THE AUSTRALIAN

Total mining output in 1945 was worth some $A65 million; in 1960 the figure was over $A362 million and in 1970 $A1,400 million. The estimate based on contracts for 1980 is $A1,877 million; further developments could possibly double that. But what does it all mean for the average citizen? The figures doubtless give some feeling of security in an era when the old mainstay of wool has seemed to be weakening. And he is much more likely than the average Briton to have personal knowledge of the stock exchange, for dabbling in shares is quite a national pastime. But he is just as likely to have lost as won in the frenzied trading of recent years.

If he is prepared for the heat and grime he can join the relatively small mining force of 45,000 and earn good money; this is how quite a few migrants start life in Australia. The remote mining townships are interesting communities. The oldest is Broken Hill; 700 miles from its state capital and 300 miles from Adelaide, it lies on the fringes of settlement in wide arid plains of saltbush on the desert edge. A land burning under 100°F (38°C) for weeks on end, of dust storms and droughts. Almost a law unto itself, Broken Hill is virtually controlled by the mining trade union, the Barrier Council; it is the town featured in the recent film *Outback*. Kalgoorlie on the other side of the desert heart has a similar reputation for tough self reliance; its water is piped from a coastal reservoir and it, too, is swept by storms of dust from the desert. In the far north, Mt Isa is the third of the older mining centres, spreading across the spinifex and rocks of the interior, its lifeline 600 miles of narrow gauge track to Townsville. The new mining towns of the 1960s, Weipa, Nhulunbuy, Tom Price and others, have forsaken the old corrugated iron idiom for air conditioned brick houses; and there is much emphasis on amenities. But labour turnover is still high.

The small but growing conservation movement is concerned at the apparent rape of the continent, while the thinking citizen wonders whether his country is becoming a vast quarry for Japan. For the Aborigines the mineral era has seen the invasion of the last of their lands, to which it has been legally stated they have in fact no title (see page 19). While there are various promises of consultation and of Aborigines being offered equities in new developments, it seems clear that the first

Australians will be the last to reap rewards from the mineral wealth of the country.

OTHER INDUSTRIES

The motor industry employs over 200,000 people in Melbourne, Adelaide and Sydney. Five major companies, Ford, Holden, British Leyland Australia, Volkswagen and Valiant (Chrysler), make 90 per cent of the cars, a total of over 400,000 vehicles a year. All the companies are overwhelmingly overseas owned. General Motors—Holden took over the original Australian Holden company and in 1948 produced their first specifically Australian car. About 35 per cent of home sales are Holdens, and there is some export. The main factory is in Melbourne; Ford operates at Geelong and in Melbourne, Chrysler in Adelaide and British Leyland in Sydney. Volkswagen, which has had a great run of success with its small tough cars, is based in Melbourne. Imported Japanese cars took 18 per cent of the market in 1971, and Japanese and French manufacturers are also assembling cars in Australia. Australian manufacturers pressing for more protection may gain by stringent regulations about the locally made content of new cars.

The processing of foodstuffs and other agricultural produce employs a large number of people, many of them seasonally in canneries or vineyards areas, and in the sugar growing regions. These activities disperse some of the industrial opportunities from the main cities, but the labour and markets of the large population centres keep flour milling and brewing in the bigger towns.

Clothing manufacture employs 112,000 people and is spread over about 4,000 establishments, with a considerable home based 'rag trade' of garment making in Sydney and Melbourne. Shoes are another industry using small workshops, especially in the inner suburbs of Melbourne. The textile industry is characterised by the production of wool, silk and cotton by one firm in one centre; but there are also some large vertically integrated factories making wool or cotton through all its processes. Here, too, there is some dispersion to the bigger towns in the country areas.

Chemical manufacture has increased rapidly with the petro-chemical industry, and will grow further with the development of natural gas and oil in Victoria. There is a large demand for fertilisers and super phosphates are produced in a number of smaller ports such as Port Lincoln and Geraldton. The drift to industrial employment from the depressed rural industries is likely to continue and to swell further the capital cities. Pleas for the decentralisation of more industry have been increasing, and both New South Wales and Victoria have schemes of financial inducement to create new factories away from Sydney and Melbourne. Success has so far been very limited.

THE RURAL SCENE

Although under 10 per cent of the workforce is engaged on the land, rural industries still account for the greater part of Australian exports. But this pattern is rapidly changing as minerals increase and the markets for wheat and wool fluctuate. There is an air of uncertainty in the Australian countryside, a feeling of having been abandoned after a century and a half of being the economic mainstay of the country.

Of some 1,200 million acres used for primary production, 93 per cent is grazing land left largely in its natural state. In parts, the quality is improved by fertilisers spread from light aircraft. Another 4 per cent is grazing land consisting of sown pastures of clovers and grasses. This leaves only 3 per cent, which is cropped. Yet crops, dominated by wheat, provide 45 per cent of the farm output by value. In the export table, wool, wheat and meat head the list.

The big sheep and cattle stations of the outback, rolling grass-lands, gum trees, boundary riders in wide brimmed hats, and scattered homesteads still exist of course and are the elements of the Australian image. The flying doctor, two way radio, rodeo and road trains are real and vital in the life of people scattered thinly over the outback. But more sheep are reared in a belt of mixed smaller farms along with wheat, than on the big inland properties; and there is an irrigated cattle farm outside Melbourne with more beasts than most of the colossal runs up north. The trend towards intensifying farming on the wetter margins of the country is likely to increase as the wide rangelands become steadily more eroded through drought and overgrazing.

Wool prices declined in recent years; incomes have been squeezed thinner between rising costs and dropping prices. The wool farmer used to boast the only unsubsidised rural product; now that a measure of government help has become necessary, he has accepted his 'deficiency payment' with some bitterness. By mid-1972 an upward trend had become established and reached boom proportions by the end of the year; but there are still fears of competition from synthetic fibres and of further recessions. Merinos provide 75 per cent of the clip; carefully protected for 150 years, the export embargo on rams was eased in 1970, to bring an immediate outcry.

Of about 20 million head of cattle, two-thirds are reared for beef and one-third for dairy products. Cattle in the tropical northern grasslands run half wild over vast unfenced properties. The Aboriginal stockman is the mainstay of an industry largely owned by absentee landlords, usually Australian or overseas companies. The animals reach the meatworks at the ports after a fattening period in coastal pastures; much of the beef is destined for the American beefburger. Australia is now the leading world exporter of beef. Australians get their beef steaks more often from the sleeker animals of the better watered country of the south-east: the Hunter valley or the hill slopes of the Divide. New cattle country is being developed in Victoria, South Australia and Western Australia by remedying minor soil deficiencies with the addition of 'trace elements' like cobalt.

The development of the tropical north of Australia for more intensive production is frequently debated. The Ord River irrigation scheme in Western Australia, the improvement of pastures elsewhere by planting new types like Townsville lucerne, and the growing of sorghum for cattle and of cotton are examples of what can be done. But many argue that the large investment involved could be more profitably employed in the temperate south. The old urge to populate the north as a defensive policy makes no sense in the nuclear age; but the proximity of the overpopulated Asian countries to an empty northern Australia does cause some qualms of conscience, if not of fear.

Dairying is confined to the wetter coastal pastures and to limited irrigated areas along the Murray. It has long been supported by subsidy, and on the marginal types of land makes a poor livelihood. A reconstruction scheme sponsored by the government now aims at helping the small farmer to change his occupation, but it is a difficult transition to make; apart from problems of re-orientation the rural areas have little employ- ment to offer. The devaluation of sterling and the proposed British entry into the European Economic Community depress the industry still further.

Wheat growing enjoyed a period of rapid expansion in the period 1955–66, buoyed up by high demand which seemed to be expanding especially in exports to China. Since then, over- production has been accompanied by a contraction in the market. Quotas were imposed on growers causing not a little hardship, especially to the newer and smaller farmers. Wheat is sold through a marketing board. The wheat growing belt forms a crescent of country across the south-east and south- west in the 10–25in rainfall zone. The smooth, rolling topo- graphy of the inland slopes and plains and the shortage of labour encouraged mechanisation early, and today armies of combine harvesters march over vast paddocks in the early summer. Grain silos are a feature of the flat landscapes along the railways that form a network across the wheat lands.

Intensively cropped land is confined to the wet coastal margins and to the interior lowlands where irrigation is avail- able. Sugar cane makes a splash of brilliant green along the eastern edge of Queensland and in the river valleys of northern

New South Wales. The gangs of cane cutters are all but gone and mechanical harvesters have taken their place. The drama of burning cane fields still lights the night sky as the 'trash' or undergrowth is cleared. The future of sugar too is clouded by the Common Market negotiations and the expiry of international agreements. Home consumers pay higher prices, which subsidise exports. Production, prices and quotas are rigidly controlled through stipulated 'mill peaks' and 'farm peaks' each year. Refining, with one exception (the Millaquin Company at Bundaberg) is in the hands of the large Colonial Sugar Refining Company, which is now spreading its interests into minerals. Exports are handled at east coast ports like Cairns or Mackay by bulk methods.

Along the Murray valley the waters from the Snowy Mountain Scheme irrigate fruit farms and sheep and cattle pastures. Fruits for the main part are canned or dried, but some grapes are blended for wine. The home of Australian brandy is along the sunny South Australian section of the Murray. South Australia grows 43 per cent of Australian vines and two-thirds are made into wines; the rest are dried. The most prized wines come from the rain-watered and not the irrigated vineyards. Some are in the hills behind Adelaide. There are also pockets of high quality wine production along the Hunter valley slopes, in parts of Victoria and on the banks of the Swan in Western Australia. The quality is kept more stable than that of European wines because the summers are more reliable. The best are hard to beat anywhere, but not much of high quality is exported. The good and reasonably cheap table wines are not least among the pleasures of living in Australia.

The citrus growers of the Murray valley face problems of increasing soil salinity, brought about by inadequate drainage of irrigation waters. The apple industry, which has made Tasmania so well known, faces problems of marketing, while still benefiting from the seasonal reversal of the southern hemisphere. Australian apples appear in British shops from about March. The imposition of levies and later tariffs by Britain is likely to prove a setback to the Australian farmer.

The most severe fluctuations to which all primary producers are subject through fluctuating prices are at least modified by the widespread use of marketing boards. Losses are cushioned by price support systems which are paid for partly by the tax payer, partly by the consumer and partly from levies on the producer. The total annual cost of farming subsidies is about $A300 million a year.

Even with this massive injection there has been a rural recession, seen in the decay of small rural townships and the depopulation of the countryside, shown by the 1971 census to be accelerating.

THE WAGE EARNER'S WORLD

In 1970 well over half the workforce of wage and salary earners belonged to one of the country's 319 trade unions; over 90 per cent are members of the relatively small group of nation-wide unions. Labour relations have a long history of organisation which has seen a lot of bitter struggle. Now they are legally protected and are part of a unique, compulsory arbitration system. The supreme labour organisation is the Australian Council of Trade Unions, which acts on behalf of the great majority of wage earners.

Arbitration in industrial disputes between employers and employees was one of the powers given to the Commonwealth by the constitution. It is compulsory for unions registered with the Commonwealth Conciliation and Arbitration Commission (and this means the representatives of 80 per cent of all union members) to take part in the arbitration procedure. The findings of the Commission are legally binding. An award in any dispute effectively becomes national and may affect wages, holidays or working conditions; it may even include a 'no strike' clause. Some 45 per cent of the workforce is affected by such legally binding Commonwealth awards and another 45 per cent by state awards.

The key event of the workers' year is the 'national wage case' and the subsequent award which in Australia is described as being 'handed down'. This becomes an automatic wage increase for all workers directly under the jurisdiction of the Commission. The state Commissions almost invariably follow suit. The concept of a 'basic wage' dates back to a famous judgement made in 1907 in the case of workers at the Massey Sunshine Harvester factory outside Melbourne. Justice Higgins laid down that no man should be paid less than enough 'to fulfil the normal needs of the average employee regarded as a human being in a civilised society'. This noble concept has had to be trimmed to the realities of what the community can afford to pay. In 1931 at the depth of the depression the basic wage was actually cut by 10 per cent.

Secondary wage payments or margins for special skills, unpleasant or dangerous work and so on, were added to the basic wage to make up a minimum wage for any occupation. In 1967 this structure was abandoned in favour of a 'total wage' award. Until 1953 the basic wage was automatically linked to the cost of living index, making an inflationary spiral of wages chasing prices an inevitable process. Since this was abandoned, the rate of increase in wages has varied; and the machinery is a very useful device in the control of inflation.

Australia has a wide variety of animals and birds. The koala is perhaps the country's best loved native animal. It is only half an inch long at birth, and stays in its mother's pouch without emerging until it is about five months old. These are in the famous koala sanctuary near Brisbane, Queensland.

A female Great Grey kangaroo with a young 'joey' in her pouch. The young, about an inch long when born, live and are suckled in the mother's pouch until ready to fend for themselves. Kangaroos and wallabies (a small species of kangaroo) are found in many parts of the continent.

Recent awards have reached 6 per cent, which to economists and politicians seem alarmingly high. But over the last decade as a whole the general rate of inflation has been much lower than in other western countries, and this is attributed to the lower rate of wage increase. 'Over award' payments are—or have been—common in a labour hungry market, but there was serious industrial trouble in 1967 when employers wanted to absorb the Commission's awarded increase into existing 'over award' payments; the move was defeated.

It is another Australian paradox that such well unionised workers should have accepted for so long what is in effect a national incomes policy, while in other nations, the very concept is anathema. There are plenty of strikes in Australia, in industry and even occasionally in postal and teaching services. Up to 1970, proportionally more working days were lost in a year than in Britain through industrial action, though less than in the United States. But with notable exceptions like the prolonged strike in Mt Isa in 1963, they are of relatively short duration.

Several explanations are offered for the general acceptance of the arbitration system. One is that it is relatively easy to find work with good 'over award' payments, overtime is easy to

―――――

Australian and Asian students under the Colombo Plan and other education programmes lunch on the lawn outside Winthrop Hall, University of Western Australia, in Perth. The University is on a picturesque site of about 165 acres on a bay of the Swan Estuary.

A reminder of Australia's position, which is fundamental to its nature. If the country did not lie athwart the Tropic, it would have few of its unique physical (and hence human) characteristics.

G

come by, and a good many have more than one job. A common practice is to own a milk, paper or bread round and also to have a full-time paid job, but full employment and overtime depends on enough consumer demand to keep factories at full stretch; this in turn is geared to the real purchasing power of the public, the control of cost inflation through wages and prices. There is no doubt of the Australian worker's capacity for militant action should these outlets for higher earning seem threatened or should he be convinced that his lot can be improved or justice done only by this means. Yet the arbitration system seems to work in the main and to be accepted. And this has been achieved without government intervention apart from the appointment of the Commissioners, whose integrity has never been questioned. Nor are the economists consulted, somewhat to their chagrin. The whole process takes the form of an inquiry by legally trained Commissioners hearing evidence from all parties; and the submission of the workers' case is the major contribution made by the trade unions to the world of their members.

THE WORKING WOMAN

The economic status of women at work and the responsibility given to them are not good. There has been trade union opposition to their employment. Only in 1966 was the Commonwealth public service opened to married women. Australia did not ratify the International Labour Organisation's declared principle of 'equal pay for equal work' made in 1951. There is a very slow move towards equality and more progress has been made in New South Wales, South Australia and Tasmania than elsewhere. A number of recent awards have stipulated equal pay and in 1972 all teachers should be in this position.

The reluctance to grant equal pay for equal work has some roots in the Harvester Judgement, for this was specifically related to the needs of a married man with two children. There is also a feeling that on the whole women have fewer responsibilities. For instance, every year hundreds of young Australian girls pack up and go overseas on working holidays, while the more earnest male must settle down to a long haul in a secure career. And in many ways it is still very much a man's country; women themselves are prepared to defend their lower economic status. At least they will be employed because they cost less; if they cost the same, they would stand little chance against a male competitor, no matter how able they were.

The greatest proportion of working women is in clerical jobs (30 per cent); 16 per cent work in factories, 13 per cent as shop assistants, and the remaining 1 per cent in various other jobs. The proportion of women in the workforce has not risen as much as might be thought in this century. In 1901, 20·5 per cent of women worked; in 1961 the proportion was 24·8 per cent. But the age and status of women had changed: the age had increased and the proportion married rose from 11 to 42 per cent. The implications are that women stay longer at school and college, work for a few years and return to work when the children are old enough.

THE WIDER WORLD OF TRADE AND TARIFF

The 'take home pay' and what it will buy, the job prospects and conditions of work, the length of holiday and the nature of the boss, these are the immediate concerns of the worker in Australia as everywhere. But of course they depend ultimately on the health of the economy as a whole, on the government's housekeeping in balancing internal problems of inflation and unemployment with the external problems of earning enough to buy imports that are wanted. The Australian record in the 1950s and the early 1960s was not very good in this respect. But in the last decade, she has managed to maintain almost full employment in the face of considerable fluctuations in the prices achieved by her exports. At the same time she kept the rate of inflation remarkably low.

	Consumer price rise (per cent)		Unemployment (per cent workforce)
	1960–9	1969–70	1960–9
Australia	2·3	3·3	1·5
USA	2·4	6·0	4·8
West Germany	2·4	3·9	1·0
Canada	2·7	3·6	5·1
France	3·4	5·6	1·5
UK	3·7	5·9	2·0
Italy	3·7	4·8	3·0
Sweden	3·8	8·9	1·3
Japan	5·5	8·1	1·1

Source: W. A. Ellis, *The Australian Economy Today*,
Lloyds Bank Review, April 1971, No 100, p 30

The policy of industrialisation which has been deliberately followed since federation led to the erection of high tariff barriers, still among the highest in the world. They cost the country some $A2,700 million a year, almost ten times the cost of support for agriculture. The tariff for individual industries at present is: motor vehicles 67 per cent; clothing 74 per cent; metal manufactures 80 per cent; furniture 55 per cent; machinery 50 per cent. Many of the very high tariffs date from the unhappy depression period of the 1930s and there is a growing feeling that a fundamental review is needed. The Commonwealth Tariff Board, an independent but government appointed body, hears and adjudicates on requests for protection. There is no doubt that many inefficient concerns are protected by the warm blanket of tariffs against the chill winds of economic reality. But the unemployment and bankruptcies that would follow more selective applications of tariffs make it almost politically impossible. It raises problems, however, in external trade, especially with Japan, now Australia's major trading partner, who naturally looks for markets in return for her enormous purchases of Australian minerals.

There was considerable pessimism about the country's trading position in the 1950s. The 1960s brought the mining miracle and in 1964 Japan ousted Britain as chief trading partner and by 1969 was taking 20 per cent of Australia's exports, while supplying 7–8 per cent of her imports. The long-standing trade agreement with Britain ends in February 1973 with the withdrawal of preferences. In 1972 Japan was taking nearly 30 per cent of Australian exports, the USA 12 per cent and Britain less than 9 per cent.

The paradoxical position of an industrialised nation which is still nevertheless dependent on primary raw materials for exports is recognised in the placing of Australia in a mid-way position in regard to international agreements through the General Agreement on Tariffs and Trade (GATT). In 1971 Australia became a member of the Organisation for Economic Co-operation and Development (OECD), which was set up in 1961 and is a body of developed nations; her rating was then twelfth as a trading nation and eighth in gross national product. There is still a balance of payments deficit, likely to disappear with the realisation of mineral contracts. The government's campaigns for increased manufacturing exports bring but slow results. The obvious markets are in south-east Asia; but these can only grow as the countries develop economically, so Australia has more than a humanitarian interest in being generous with her foreign aid.

Along with low unemployment and relatively low rates of inflation, however, Australia shows a rather low growth rate in the 1960s of 2 per cent (UK 2·3, West Germany 4, Japan 8, USA 2·8). Labour productivity did not increase very much. One reason suggested is that there are not enough differentials in wage structures to allow for a pool of skilled workers. Another is the protection of inefficient industries and a third the high cost of educating and housing a migrant in relation to his initial productivity. In addition the size of the country leads to enormous internal transport costs, and her isolation to heavy freight charges on ocean cargoes. The home market is small and does not allow for 'economies of scale'. But in the 1970s it is becoming clear that economic growth pays a very heavy price in environmental damage; where living standards are already high, perhaps it need not matter if growth is not dramatic. The rate is forecast to accelerate in the 1970s to 5–7 per cent; this would represent a 3 per cent increase in living standards given the successful management of inflationary processes.

This does not seem quite so hopeful in 1972 as it did in 1970. The last quarter of 1971 showed an increase in the cost of living that would amount to 9·2 per cent a year. And in January 1972, unemployment was the highest in ten years, with 2·3 per cent of the workforce affected. There have been reports of cut backs in steel production, of shift reduction and the laying off of car workers. A Japanese recession in industry associated with a drop in her exports to America is leading her to put brakes on some of her vast overseas mineral undertakings: coal in Queensland has already been affected in the delay of the big Nebo project inland from Mackay; the huge new copper mine in New Guinea may have to curtail production; lead production has been reduced at Mt Isa. And at Paraburdoo, south-west of Tom Price in Western Australia, there are unfinished houses and a new school with no pupils, and work has been suspended even on the brewery, a bad sign in this hot and thirsty land. The mine designed to tap some 700 million tons of iron ore is lying disused. Hamersley Iron has agreed to vary its contracts with Japan, and expects to be given priority when the demand for iron increases again.

Australians also worry to some extent over the proportion of overseas ownership of mining and industrial undertakings, and even land holding. The inflow of foreign capital has to find an appropriate outflow of profits; how much does Australia benefit from the economic activities it generates within the country? By 1975 well over half the companies operating in Australia will be foreign owned. In February 1972 a Premiers' Conference resulted in an 'injection' of $A90 million into the economy in the form of grants to the states; New South Wales took $A40 million. It was hoped that by this and other measures to alleviate rural depression, the disquieting drift might be halted. But if Australia has indeed reached the top of the hill, it is fervently to be hoped that there will be no fast run down the other side; for the broad back of the sheep may not always be there to take the strain.

6

How They Learn

THE educational system in Australia retains family likenesses to its British parents, but has also many features of its own determined by history and environment, and has incorporated some of the North American approach as well. Education is primarily the responsibility of the states, so there are six separate systems, each centrally controlled from the state capital under a Minister and Department of Education and through a Director or Director-General. The variations of curricula and examinations cause difficulties for families moving inter-state. But there is considerable uniformity within each state system; a common criticism is that excessive control from the centre leads as it were to a 'regimental slow march' through the set curricula. A second criticism is of the generally authoritarian character of Australian education, extending right down through the hierarchy to the final teacher-pupil relationship. There is historical reason for this, developing from the birth of the six colonies under quasi-military authority and extending outwards from single, dominant port capitals. The Commonwealth has come to take an increasing interest in education through the Commonwealth Department of Education and Science, set up in 1966. But apart from some financial help for schools, the main Commonwealth concern is in tertiary education.

SCHOOLS

At primary and secondary level there is a three-fold system

throughout Australia: state schools educate 75 per cent of the children, a further 20 per cent attend Roman Catholic schools and the remaining 5 per cent private 'independent' schools. For the state-educated child, tuition is free, the buildings and staff are provided by the Department, but text books, library books, stationery and teaching aids as well as sports equipment are not. These must be provided by the local community, although there are varying degrees of subsidy. Most commonly, a group called the Parents' and Citizens' Association is formed for each school and acts as a fund raising organisation; activities include running a school canteen, for there is no official school dinner system.

Teachers can be posted to any school and this ensures some uniformity of teaching supply and standards for the less attractive areas. But the books and equipment clearly vary with the enthusiasm and prosperity of the community and this favours the middle class as against the poorer communities. Teachers tend not to become integrated with the community they serve because of their enforced mobility; this can operate to the detriment of both.

Some 20,000 children who live too far from a district school even to use the free school bus service work through Correspondence schools to the end of secondary school stage. Their work is supervised by a parent and posted to the capital. Correspondence courses are supplemented by twelve Schools of the Air which between them serve 12 million square miles. Using two way radio, children are linked with each other and with their teacher. While a few may suffer from missing formal all day schooling, on the whole they compare very favourably with their peers in later performance.

Educational costs borne by the parent are allowed as a deductable expense in income tax returns. They include uniform, text books, exercise books, and any fees charged. State schools may charge a fee that covers the use of books; Roman Catholic schools charge tuition fees, although these may be waived in primary schools in poorer areas.

Finance and the control of schooling have been a constant

source of bitterness and controversy in Australia between church and state and church and church. In the early days there was strong dependence on religious bodies for providing education; this fitted in with the general nineteenth century opinion that the main aim was moral training. In the early days of expanding settlement, government help was needed and varying forms of dual control between church and state evolved. But as the six colonies (New South Wales, Tasmania, Victoria, Queensland, South Australia and Western Australia) achieved self government there rose a cry for 'free, compulsory and secular education'. Acts passed between 1872 and 1893 established a pattern which is maintained in the six states that succeeded the old colonies at federation. The refusal of state aid to church schools that the policy entailed roused bitterest opposition among the Roman Catholics.

A higher proportion of Catholic children are educated in church schools in Australia than in Britain or America. The reason is historical, and is related to the high proportion of Irish in the Australian Catholic population. With a legacy of distrust of the Protestant English, they felt that the only way to protect their religious beliefs from dilution and disregard was to keep the children under their own moral and educational surveillance. They point out that by doing so they save the tax payer the costs of 20 per cent of the total educational bill for the country; why then should they not expect some financial help? After close on a century of controversy, the Commonwealth made the first move towards state aid in 1963 by offering help to all independent secondary schools for the provision of science teaching facilities; this was later extended to libraries. It has been followed by the introduction of two-year Commonwealth scholarships awarded by examination to about the top 10 per cent of fifteen year olds, whether at state or private school and without any means test. It is worth $A400 a year to a private school pupil, less to a state school child. The states have followed suit and now provide some sort of financial help to independent schools, usually in the form of a grant per pupil.

It is factual, if also cynical, to point out that the clear victory of the Liberal/Country Party coalition in 1963 was linked to their offer of state aid, for Roman Catholics represent 25 per cent of the voters. It is now accepted and no political party would survive the ending of it. But there remains some resentment among the educationalists who deplore the replication of scarce educational facilities in every community, whether or not it is economic in relation to size.

The school year runs from late January or early February to mid-December, with shorter holidays in May and August, a weekend at Easter and the public holidays. Full-time education usually begins at five, although it is not compulsory until six, and ends at fifteen in all states but Tasmania where the leaving age is sixteen. The needs of the three to four year olds are rather poorly provided for, save in favoured places like Canberra where the Commonwealth provides beautiful 'pre-schools'. Tasmania's Department of Education runs a system of pre-schools; the Commonwealth looks after Northern Territory and provides one 'Lady Gowrie' pre-school in each state capital. For the rest, such pre-schools as exist are organised by voluntary bodies which enjoy varying measures of state assistance.

Primary schools in Australia are dedicated fairly explicitly to developing the basic skills with words and numbers. They are subject also to quite strict discipline even of the youngest. Teachers for state primary schools are trained over a two year course in colleges run by the Department; the period is being increased to three years. Transfer of pupils to secondary schools is automatic at twelve (thirteen in Queensland).

The secondary system varies with the states but the commonest type of school is comprehensive and co-educational and serves a specific catchment area. Selection was important in New South Wales until the introduction in the 1960s of the Wyndham Scheme, which aims at catering for the whole ability range in one school by providing three levels of study in each subject during the six years of the secondary course. Comprehensive education is also the rule in Tasmania and Western Australia. Victoria has a dual structure of technical schools and more academically oriented high schools, with entry dependent so far as possible on parental choice. Some form of selection is retained in Queensland and in South Australia. In all states there are agricultural high schools, generally with high reputations and combining rural skills with liberal studies. The varying structure of external examinations is given in the table on p 118, but in general there is a lower certificate for the fifteen year olds about to leave and who still make up 75 per cent of the secondary pupils, and a later matriculating examination heavily influenced by university requirements.

Only about half of the teachers in secondary schools have a university degree when they begin, although a good many work externally to obtain one. Education Departments recruit largely through a system of bonding: fees and maintenance are paid to qualified students who undertake legally to teach for a given period at whatever school to which the authority appoints them. They may use the grant for university or college courses; but it is difficult for them to take a longer Honours course. As a public servant the teacher is restricted in his individual freedom to express his views, but as a trade union teachers are quite militant and have taken strike action. The centralised organisation can be inhibiting for a gifted teacher with an individual approach; the authoritarian tradition makes it equally difficult to break down the fairly overt hostility between teachers and pupils where control is exercised rather more by discipline than respect.

In the independent schools the authoritarian element is every bit as marked; nor do they often take advantage of the freedom to develop their own educational methods, since they are geared to the same set of external examinations as the state schools. Roman Catholic secondary schools are often run by particular religious orders; some are as prestigious as the non-Catholic independent schools. There are seventy-seven boys' schools identified by membership of the Australian Headmasters' Conference (a direct parallel with the British Headmasters' Conference), and a further ninety-one girls' schools with an equivalent earmark. Of the boys' schools, twenty-three are in Victoria, long the chief bastion of private education; whether a reason for or a result of the somewhat mediocre standards of the state schools there, it is hard to say. Of the eight 'Great Public Schools' four are in Victoria. The total includes Geelong Grammar, which, like King's School Parammatta in Sydney, has always had strong links with the landed 'squattocracy'. Scotch College, Melbourne, is a Presbyterian establishment once described as the biggest Public School in the British Empire; it has a formidable record of academic achievement. Many subsequent leaders are educated at the Public Schools; again one is chary of distinguishing cause and effect. Enough of the higher echelons in politics, industry, civil service and military forces come from them to represent another Australian paradox: that of a professedly egalitarian society encouraging the purchase of privilege through private education.

HIGHER EDUCATION

Well over half a million people are engaged in some form of tertiary education each year, 80 per cent of them part-time. About 22 per cent are university students of whom half are part-timers, 6 per cent are undergoing teacher training, 23 per cent technical training and 21 per cent courses connected with a particular trade. The remainder are engaged in courses covering school syllabuses commercial subjects, agriculture, art, music and military studies. The vast majority are motivated by the career prospects to be gained from further qualifications. As in schools there has been a great post-war expansion brought about both by population growth and an expanding technical economy. Two very influential reports have been the Murray Report on the Universities (1958) and the Martin Report on the Future of Tertiary Education (1965).

State or Territory	Title and year of secondary examinations	Universities with date of foundation
New South Wales	School Certificate (4) Higher School Certificate (6)	Sydney 1850 New England 1954 New South Wales 1958 Newcastle 1965 Macquarie 1967 Wollongong University Collge 1962 (attached to University of New South Wales)
Victoria	Intermediate School Certificate (4) Higher School Certificate (6)	Melbourne 1853 Monash 1958 La Trobe 1967
Queensland	Junior Public (3) Senior Public (5) (Entry to secondary school at 13 not 12)	Queensland 1909 James Cook University of North Queensland 1970 Griffith 1971
South Australia	Intermediate School Certificate (3) Matriculation (5)	Adelaide 1874 Flinders 1966
Western Australia	Achievement Certificate awarded on school leaving with accumulated credits	Western Australia 1909 Murdoch 1971
Tasmania	School Certificate (4) Higher School Certificate (5-6)	Tasmania 1890
Northern Territory	Schools administered by South Australia	Nil
Australian Capital Territory	Schools administered by New South Wales	Australian National University 1946 (Reorganised 1960)

THE UNIVERSITIES

About 10 per cent of the relevant age group begin a university course each year, more than in Britain. It has been easy on the whole to gain admission through matriculation, although in recent years some quota systems have been introduced. Some 45 per cent of students have financial assistance, 27 per cent of these with Commonwealth scholarships awarded on performance in school leaving certificates. The scholarship covers fees; maintenance grants are based on a fairly stringent means test which excludes two-thirds of the holders. The other scholarships are almost all awards under the bonding system already described for teachers, and widely used by firms, public authorities and so on. Australia has an exceptionally high number of students financed in this way, at least compared with other wealthy nations: a UNESCO survey showed that of fourteen nations classed as wealthy eleven gave students aid with no strings attached.

While the entry rate is high, the proportion of students who drop out of courses before completion or who fail at the end of it is depressingly high too. A survey of 10,000 students showed that 32 per cent of full-time students dropped out and 63 per cent of part-time students. Of the survivors only 50 per cent of the part-timers passed their final examinations. There are probably two main factors: the commendable Australian philosophy of 'giving it a go' leads many to start a course who simply do not have the bent or ability; and the financial problems are also important. In addition the part-time student may face real social and family problems in maintaining a balance between home, job and private study.

Nevertheless, the large classes typical of an Australian university are likely to contain a higher proportion of really promising students than a comparable group in an English provincial university. This is partly at least because the highly gifted are not 'creamed off' as they are in England to the old universities of Oxford and Cambridge. Universities are the concern of the states and students tend to go to their own local university, as in the older Scottish tradition. The table summarises the names and dates of foundation of the universities today. Before World War II there were six, one in each state capital; now there are seventeen. The first universities were set up in the late nineteenth and early twentieth centuries and owed much in style to the British provincial universities of the same era; many staff members were recruited in Britain. In 1946 the Commonwealth established the Australian National University in Canberra as a post-graduate research institution with a primary objective of attracting back to the country some of her outstanding expatriate scholars. In this aim the ANU has been highly successful and has also achieved international repute in a number of fields of research. In 1960 the ANU was reorganised to take in the former Canberra University College (until then associated with the University of Melbourne) to form an undergraduate wing. Following the Murray Report there has been a rapid growth of new universities in the states. The University of New South Wales in Sydney is strongly oriented towards applied sciences and technology. The University of New England at Armidale in the far north of New South Wales has two-thirds of its students working externally, and attending short compulsory residential courses. But the state capitals continue to dominate: the James Cook University at Townsville in Queensland, and Newcastle and New England Universities in New South Wales are the only ones outside state capitals.

Commonwealth financial help is now essential for the universities. It is administered through the Australian Universities Commission, whose grants are made each triennium. The amount given must be matched by the state governments, and this is where troubles begin; state politicians are not notably keen about universities or students.

It seems likely that the student population explosion will ease in the 1970s now that the post-war 'bulge' has passed through and there are new avenues of tertiary education opening up. This, it is suggested, should give the universities time to pause, consolidate and give thought to the quality of their teaching. Staff-student ratios have tended to be poor, leading to large anonymous groups receiving lectures but not enough tutorial work. The research by teachers which is needed to fertilise their teaching has also suffered from lack of funds. The states have been very jealous of the ANU Research Schools in this respect. The general attitude that universities should primarily be 'service stations' on the climb up the ladder of career promotion has been seen by critics as stultifying more creative approaches; but it would be a utopian society that saw them today as academic ivory towers. And there has been a considerable improvement in funds for research with a faster increase in this field than in the reduction of classes.

OTHER TERTIARY EDUCATION

The Martin Report urged the diversification of tertiary education to divert some of the flow of matriculated school leavers into more appropriate channels than universities. And this is now taking place through the strengthening of existing centres of technical education and through the creation of about a dozen new Colleges of Advanced Education. Some have been specially built, like the fine new campus in Canberra; others have been upgraded from existing institutions. Colleges of Advanced Education offer vocational training and a range of liberal studies, but are not likely to award degrees. In 1969 close on 40,000 students were at such colleges; half the total are in Victoria.

Technical education is mainly handled by the state Education Departments; New South Wales has a separate Department of Technical Education. But there are increasing moves towards handling higher education through Councils, Boards or Authorities of Higher Education. Although there are several old and well trusted technical colleges (as in Sydney) that have turned out generations of engineers, architects and so on, the field of technical education has been the poor relation. Industry

H

has been largely derivative and Australian innovation largely confined to the agricultural side. On the other hand there has always been a shortage of skilled labour and this has been the main province of technical training. Well over 90 per cent of technical education is undertaken part time. The professional qualification, sought by about 10 per cent, is usually a diploma. Day release has been well established for some years and there are a number of sandwich courses; but evening classes are the principal approach. Full-time students have increased since 1965 when Commonwealth scholarships became available. In most states technical education follows a normal school period; but Victoria has a system of technical high schools. Commonwealth help has been extended to outright grants for buildings and matching grants on the pattern of university grants to the states.

ADULT EDUCATION

Formal adult education, non-vocational but aiming to provide cultural outlets and personal improvement, takes the form mainly of evening classes. These are run by the universities, by Education Departments and by the voluntary Workers' Education Association, inspired by the British organisation of the same name, but receiving less support in Australia. In adult education the capital cities again have the great advantage and although funds have been scarce there has been notable work done. The Adult Tutorial Class in Sydney University, for instance, has prompted the production of the very high standard *Current Affairs Bulletin*.

Only about 1 per cent of adults are estimated to be attending non-vocational evening classes. As in other industrial and increasingly automated societies leisure time is bound to increase. Whether this will send more Australians to the beach or the blackboard would not perhaps be too hard to prophesy, for the sun-given euphoria of sand and surf is very seductive.

EDUCATION AND SOCIETY

Educational spending accounts for under 5 per cent of the gross national product, which is low in comparison with countries at a similar state of development. To some extent this may reflect Australian attitudes, which are suspicious of the 'clever bloke', although the top people in law and the professions command great respect. The lower rungs of academics and teachers do not have a high standing in society. The increased spending that will be needed to keep the country geared to the times will present politicians with a challenging task.

7

How They Get About

WITH a car for every three people, it is obvious how most Australians get about. Looking at the total 'transport task' of the nation, it appears that 83 per cent go by road; the railways account for 13 per cent and air traffic 4 per cent. The transport system is well developed in relation to population, but the 'tyranny of distance' means long lines of communication both within Australia and with the outside world.

AIR TRANSPORT

Aviation in Australia has one of the best safety records in the world, partly the result of very strict regulations by the Commonwealth Department of Civil Aviation, but helped by the generally settled weather conditions and absence of high and rugged mountain ranges. Australia has made important contributions to aviation, from the kite flying experiments Lawrence Hargraves carried out on a beach in New South Wales in the 1890s to the fine aircraft designs of Sir Lawrence Wackett in more recent times and the record breaking flights of Kingsford Smith and others.

The isolation of settlements in the outback led to the development of commercial flying in Australia from the 1920s. The first route flown was from Geraldton to Derby in Western Australia in 1921. The original QANTAS, which stands for Queensland and Northern Territories Aerial Services Limited, began flights between Cloncurry and Charleville in Queensland in 1922. The first inter-capital flights began in 1930 between Brisbane and Sydney and soon extended to Melbourne and Hobart. The disappearance of the *Southern Cloud* over the Australian Alps in 1931 put a damper on development for a time (the wreckage was not found until 1958 during work on the Snowy Mountains Scheme).

Meantime QANTAS Empire Airways had been formed in 1934 to run the Singapore-Sydney leg of the London-Australia route. Today QANTAS is an international airline of world class, covering over 80,000 miles of unduplicated route miles a year and carrying over a quarter of a million passengers, almost half the total entering or leaving the country. It is entirely Commonwealth owned.

Internal flying is divided between public and private undertakings. The post-war Labor government wanted to nationalise internal airways completely, but this was declared unconstitutional under Section 92 of the Constitution which had been written to ensure complete freedom of trade between the states. Trans Australia Airlines (TAA) is the nationalised interstate line, and in its early days it enjoyed some government support. But with the change to more conservative government this was withdrawn, in spite of which TAA has largely remained the pacemaker in internal aviation and has a very good performance. The competing private internal line is Ansett Airways. (R. M. Ansett is head of a number of business concerns, principally Ansett Transport Industries which includes the airways, freight and tourist business.)

The two airlines used to run equivalent flights on routes where traffic was deemed to justify it; the system led at times to ludicrous duplication, and has been altered. But the two-airline policy will remain for the time being. In addition each has a sphere to itself, Ansett operating mainly from Melbourne and TAA in Northern Territory, Queensland and Tasmania.

Within the states, feeder services and internal flights to the capitals and between the larger centres are largely in the indirect control of the Ansett group. Exceptions are some TAA flights, the East-West Airlines of New South Wales, centred on the northern inland town of Tamworth, and the subsidised Connellan Airline; operating out of Alice Springs, this includes remarkable aerial 'bus routes' serving isolated settlements. The smaller internal routes are served mainly by Fokker *Friendships* and *Fellowships*, the inter capital flights by *Boeing* 727 jets and *Douglas* DC9s. Some 2,000 people have their own aircraft, many of them station owners.

RAILWAYS

Railways have played an important role in the agricultural development of Australia and are now playing an equally important part in the mineral era of today. From the 1850s, rail nets spread inland from each state capital. They remain the responsibility of the states, but there is also a Commonwealth railway system. Queensland, Victoria and New South Wales had agreed to use the Irish gauge of 5ft 3in but a change in the head of the New South Wales railways led to the adoption in that state of the British gauge of 4ft 8½in instead. South Australia had a 5ft 3in gauge, so from the start Melbourne and Adelaide were not separated by a gauge break. The high costs of constructing such long lengths as were needed led to the use of the narrow 3ft 6in gauge in Queensland, Western Australia and Tasmania and in parts of South Australia. Since for many decades the chief function of the railways was to feed the state port capitals with raw materials for export, the varying gauges were not important. But with federation and the growth of inter-state traffic, the problems of exchange increased. Agreement in principle to standardise was reached as long ago as 1921. But over the next forty years the only progress made was the extension of the New South Wales standard gauge line across the border to Brisbane. New initiatives came in the 1950s and in 1962 a standard gauge line was continued from the New South Wales-Victoria border at Wodonga on the Murray to Melbourne, so getting rid of the most troublesome break of gauge between the two biggest cities. Interchangeable bogeys have also been introduced—a measure, it has been pointed out, that could have overcome the major problems long ago.

The greatest achievement has been the completion of the links allowing a continuous journey from Sydney to Perth; the new *Indian Pacific* now completes the 2,461 miles in under 70 hours. The task involved extending the standard gauge line built across the Nullarbor in 1917, by building a new standard gauge line between Kalgoorlie and Perth; in the east the line had to be standardised from Port Augusta in South Australia through Port Pirie and up to meet the New South Wales line at Broken Hill. The internal lines in the states will retain their present gauges, but it remains to bring Adelaide into the standard gauge network. Some 500 miles of standard gauge line from Alice Springs to the Trans Continental line is at the planning stage.

The great new mineral lines of Western Australia are standard gauge, but in Queensland new railways to carry coal to the coast are narrow gauge and so is the upgraded 600 miles of line that brings out Mt Isa copper to Townsville. The old North Australia Railway that set out so hopefully from Darwin for Alice Springs many years ago foundered in political and financial apathy after about 300 miles and seems unlikely to be completed, though its existing track has also been improved for ore trains. The Commonwealth Railway from the south reached Alice Springs in 1929 and the famous *Ghan* carries vehicles and passengers over the desert flats of central Australia, where fickle rivers can rise and wash out the track and sometimes strand a train for weeks.

Apart from the modern inter-city and the Trans Continental expresses, passenger travel by train is slow and tedious; in holiday periods, 'second division' trains are used and are far from comfortable. It is not surprising that on the whole long distance travellers prefer to fly, although the costs are at least a third more; while for shorter distances (in Australia that can mean up to 1,000 miles) many people prefer to drive. But the states do not want high losses on their expensive rail nets, so understandably have sought to restrict the development of road haulage.

The famous Section 92 of the Constitution has been invoked to prevent the imposition of tax on inter-state road transport, which consequently flourishes. But within the state boundaries the governments can and do strictly control long distance road haulage over 25 to 50 miles by withholding licences if there is a competing railway line that is deemed adequate, and by imposing quite heavy taxes in some cases based on tonnage. It has been known for truck drivers to hop out of one state and back again with a load to qualify for inter-state indemnity, but this has now been declared illegal. Such are the complexities that have arisen from the well intentioned efforts of the founding fathers, who were drafting their constitution before the motor or air age.

Road building began very early, using convict labour, and a net soon spread out from the main cities. But the system is now increasingly strained under the burden of carrying 80 per cent of all passengers and 75 per cent of all freight traffic. The main urban centres are linked by bitumen surfaced highways, and there is a fairly rapid development of high standard urban freeways. The new Toll Road that runs from Sydney to Newcastle cuts like a knife through the orange sandstones and across the deep Hawkesbury valley. But the Pacific Highway, which follows the coast from Sydney round to Melbourne, has some very rough patches and is occasionally cut by floods from the plateau edge where waterfalls cascade to the plain.

Of a total mileage of some 560,000 of roadway, only a fifth is bitumen surfaced; a quarter has all weather gravel, which varies in quality with the local material available. Most of the remainder comprises unsurfaced dirt roads; periodically the ruts and potholes are levelled by huge grading machines—but many of these roads are impassable in wet weather. Gravel and dirt roads are hard on vehicles, on driver and passengers too. When two cars pass, windows are hastily wound up to keep out some of the clouds of red dust churned up; front seat passenger or driver puts a hand on the windscreen to minimise damage by flying stones.

The states are responsible for their own main roads, while local roads are the concern of local authorities, in some cases a specifically elected Road Board. The Commonwealth makes annual grants to the states for road expenditure, based on population and vehicle figures. The new Development Roads of the north, built for the cattle trade largely, are financed mainly by the Commonwealth; along them pound the giant articulated road trains, filled with cattle for railheads or fattening pastures and filling with terror the motorist who encounters them.

The urban Australian prefers on the whole to go to work by car, though this may leave his wife stranded in the suburban expanses; so a second car becomes a high priority. There are electrified suburban services by rail in Sydney and Melbourne and an electric line runs out from Sydney to the Blue Mountains, taking commuters to the pleasant townships on their slopes. Melbourne still has its trams and there are urban bus services. Inter-city, the cheapest transport, is by long-distance coach, and the tourist services have fleets of air-conditioned coaches. But over Australian distances prolonged coach travel is arduous.

Traffic regulations are the responsibility of the individual states, but nationwide the rule is to keep to the left and give way to the right. The high accident rate has been touched on. Yet while it is conceded that the Australian driver may have less patience and courtesy on the road than his British counterpart, he also tends to have more compassion for the chap in trouble by the roadside. And that flair for improvisation will get many a stranded motorist on his way again.

SHIPPING

Not many Australians get about their country by water, for fairly obvious reasons. A few tourists use the revived steamer service that makes trips down the Murray for their benefit. But this is a pale ghost of the once thriving river traffic on Australia's only navigable (but unreliable) waterway. The railways choked the river traffic in its prime a hundred years ago; but with the vagaries of rivers and cargoes it has always been a chancy business.

On the other hand the bulk of the country's economic life lies within relatively easy reach of the sea and coastal shipping has had a very much longer life and is still important, but for freight not people. If the traveller wants to do the unlikely thing and sail from Sydney to Perth he must join an international ship on her way to Europe. But every year, over 120,000 tourists cross the Bass Strait to holiday in Tasmania by one of the passenger vehicle ferries of the Australian National Line sailing from Sydney and Melbourne.

Like TAA, the ANL is a flourishing publicly owned enterprise; it must be run on the lines of a private company and show a profit; it has no subsidy. The ANL is expanding into overseas trade to Japan, Europe and America, with new container vessels. Altogether the line has 34 ships and handles 45 per cent of the internal shipping freight. Another 25 per cent are handled by BHP carrying iron, coal and limestone. Coal is also brought by ship from the Hunter valley fields to Sydney by the famous old Sixty Milers, chugging down the east coast. But the coastal trade has declined heavily in face of land transport.

In the external shipping trade by which Australia must live, only 2 per cent of the tonnage involved are Australian owned; there are plans to increase this. The development of ship building was inhibited by the early monopoly of the East India Company and today labour costs would make it difficult for her to enter the field in a competitive way. There are five shipyards, but they do not produce a very high tonnage and are subsidised. Modern developments include container shipping affecting Australian ports. Special facilities have been built at Melbourne, Sydney and Fremantle. The export of bulky minerals to Japan means that many ships return in ballast in spite of an increase in return cargoes of Japanese manufactured goods. On the other hand the import of oil from the Middle East means ships going that way are often in ballast. The European trade is more evenly balanced. The passenger traffic of course has been heavily weighted by migrants on the outward run, but the Australian love of travel and the desire many still have, in spite of loosening ties, to see the 'old country' ensure a fairly constant flow in the other direction.

8

How They Amuse Themselves

LEISURE time activities in Australia are on the whole gregarious, whether in the sunshine of the great outdoors, or in the clubs and pubs. But the general reputation the country has of being a rather philistine society which rejects culture is not entirely justified. Australia has probably made as many and as important contributions to the world of the arts as to the world of sport. And while absolute numbers are of course small, the proportion of the population which cares for music, drama and arts is probably very similar to that of any other western country.

SPORT

Whether as participators, spectators or speculators, Australians love sport. As players they have a very strongly developed competitive spirit. Perhaps this is a quality developed during a history of pioneering and fortified by the infusion of migrant stock, which almost by definition is venturesome in outlook. Certainly the will to win is powerful, even aggressive at times, and is fostered by intensive, serious minded coaching. Potential champions are picked out early in club, state and national contests, and training is both disciplined and scientific. The outdoor tradition, reliable summer weather and good living standards also play their part. Schools give at least one afternoon a week to sport; but here too the concentration on talent and competition is marked, tending to overshadow such other educational functions as may be claimed for these activities.

Australia's outstanding position in the world of sport is indicated by the eight gold and seven silver medals gained at the 1972 Olympics.

International achievements by individuals are greatest in swimming and tennis. Hot summer weather makes swimming a very popular pastime from about November to March. Yet there are surprisingly few heated pools and even fewer that are indoors, in spite of the cool winters of the southern parts of the continent; except for those in training it is very much a seasonal sport. Every year there are well publicised campaigns to teach children to swim; yet every year also there are some hundreds of deaths from drowning throughout Australia. Inland, people swim in rivers and lakes and in the excavated earth dams on the grazing properties. All have their hazards for the unwary in uneven beds and layers of cold water; in some cases there is even a health hazard, or just drawbacks like the voracious leeches of some inland lakes.

Wherever possible, however, the Australian makes for the coast in summer. The sweeping bays, the rocky headlands, the endless blue of Pacific or Indian Ocean act like magnets. But here too there are some dangers to the swimmer. A savage tidal rip can develop at the ends of short curved beaches and on the long straight stretches of the coast; so the safest bays are those of medium size. In the south-west of the country waves of exceptional size called 'king waves' can roll in without warning and carry off sunbather or fisherman. The rocky platforms fringing headlands are ideal fishing sites but also take their toll of the careless or unlucky.

Sharks are a danger in sheltered estuaries and harbours but out of over ninety species only a few like the pointer, whaler, grey nurse and tiger sharks are dangerous maneaters. Here the gregarious habits of humans are a protection, since sharks keep away from splashing groups. Many frequented bays are protected by netting, and over wider areas there are shark-spotting planes and shark lookout towers. Warnings of sharks in the vicinity are sent out over loudspeakers, and then it is a case of 'everybody out' until the animals are chased off. But one is never just entirely comfortable. To round off a catalogue that may seem excessively off-putting, there can be occasional plagues of what Australians call 'bluebottles'; these are creatures known elsewhere as 'Portuguese men-of-war', and consist of a vivid blue inflated bladder from which trail long, stinging tentacles inflicting sharp pain. They are brought in by winds and currents to die in thousands along the beach, sometimes having to be cleared by bulldozers. In tropical waters the highly poisonous stonefish lie camouflaged on rocks and reefs.

In spite of all this, thousands enjoy the sea and sand in perfect safety. Their confidence is greatest in areas patrolled by the famous Life-savers. There are some 250 Life-saving Clubs with voluntary members who patrol the most frequented beaches and who have saved well over 150,000 lives this century, more than the total Australian dead in two world wars. The Life-savers use special lightweight surf boats. They also rescue people in distress by means of a length of rope which is attached at one end to a revolving drum and at the other to the 'belt-man' who then swims out and takes hold of the swimmer so that both are wound in to safety. Life-savers also man the lookout towers to watch for developing rips. They have evolved their own mystique of clubmanship based on intense physical fitness and competitive carnivals.

The Life-savers are sometimes looked on as rather comic squares by the new generation, and especially by the 'surfies'. Surf riding on the breakers of the long ocean swell that surrounds much of Australia (save where protected as by the Barrier Reef) is a passion. The long sleek boards of balsa or fibre-glass can cost $A200 or more. The group unit is important and carloads of young people will drive a hundred miles looking for a beach with the best conditions. Their sport calls for skill and daring and is beautiful to watch. 'Surfies' are sometimes denigrated as irresponsible gangs; but this is less than fair although there have indeed been some ugly incidents in clashes with authority, with rivals, with life-savers and with swimmers.

In international swimming Australia has produced world famous figures. Among them perhaps Dawn Fraser has stood supreme. Her 100 metre freestyle record set up in the 1964 Olympics was only beaten in 1971; and then by a fellow Australian only fourteen years old. Dawn had overcome early asthma to reach the top through years of hard training; her Olympic coup followed a bad car crash; this is the stuff of Australian hero worship. Yet she was debarred from competition by her own country's swimming authority following some mildly rebellious behaviour. And this too is an element in Australian sportsmanship, where discipline is all important.

The easy access to the sea makes sailing also a very popular sport. There are at least 200,000 weekend sailors and some 5,000 new boats are built each year. Sheltered estuaries and inland waterways are thick with sails in summer, including the artificial Lake Burley Griffin in Canberra where on a summer Sunday the water can scarcely be seen between them. When Sir Francis Chichester sailed into Sydney Harbour during his heroic solo round the world he was met by a huge flotilla of fellow enthusiasts. The competitive spirit finds an outlet in club and inter club racing. Ocean racing for bigger craft takes place between several major cities: best known is the annual Sydney to Hobart race which sets off on Boxing Day from Sydney; this brings international competitors who have included the present British Prime Minister, Edward Heath. Australia has been dogged but unsuccessful as a challenger for the America's Cup in 1962, 1967 and 1970.

On land, Australians are just as enthusiastic sportsmen. Tennis players have held a dominant international position over the last fifteen years. Rod Laver, born in Rockhampton in Queensland, is probably the finest tennis player the world has yet seen. In 1962 and again in 1969 he won the Grand Slam of the American, European and Wimbledon championships. John Newcombe was the 1971 Wimbledon champion. Margaret Court emerged as a champion at seventeen and went on to win Wimbledon in 1962, 1969 and 1970, and held the American title in 1969 to 1971. Today the vivid personality of Evonne Goolagong has appeared to carry on the Australian tradition by winning Wimbledon in 1971. Australia has won the international challenge competition of the Davis Cup sixteen times since 1950. The young hopefuls continue to be selected and trained, all the year round, but there is some current anxiety that spectator interest is waning in tennis, swimming and cricket. In turn this can starve the sports of funds for competitive training.

Cricket in Australia is almost as old as white settlement; both military and civilian communities had clubs by 1826. The first English team went out in 1861, and the first Australian team visited England in 1868. This was a fascinating enterprise as the entire team were Aborigines, trained by a settler in Victoria. They won fourteen, lost fourteen and drew nineteen games against English sides. But it has never been repeated. The first Test Match was played in 1877, and in 1882 Australia's first victory led to the famous *In Memoriam* which appeared in *The Times*:

> *In affectionate memory of English cricket, which died at the Oval 29th August 1882 . . . The body will be cremated and the ashes taken to Australia.*

The following year in Sydney an urn containing the ashes of a burned stump was solemnly presented to the victorious side from England and taken to the pavilion at Lord's Cricket Ground, where it has remained ever since. Australia has 'won the ashes' eighty times between 1876 and 1972, but never takes the urn home. Test Matches are followed avidly by thousands of Australians, listening to crackling commentaries at dead of night. Today cricket has been drawn into the racial issue with the halting of the South African Tests. Among a galaxy of cricketing stars Sir Donald Bradman shines supreme; his overall Test average 1928–48 only fell four runs short of the century, and his record of 1,448 runs in one season stood for thirty-one years until 1971.

Within Australia the most important cricketing trophy is the

Sheffield Shield, competed for by the six states. The quiet image of a gentleman's game has not infrequently been shattered, mainly by controversies about bowling techniques. Angry cables shot between the MCC in London and the Australians over the 'body line' debate in the 1930s, and more recently there have been scenes about alleged 'throwing'. Sydney Cricket Ground has a reputation for noisy barracking by the crowd on the slope known as The Hill.

But the more aggressive sportsmen are more likely to be found out 'hunting' than watching cricket. This consists of driving out into the bush to pot at rabbits or kangaroos. The average Australian family, however, prefers the more peaceful amusement of picnicking. It is so easy relatively to get to beach or bush, provided you do not mind your fellow men all doing the same thing, so that you all end up at the picnic spots along the more accessible routeways. To get far from the crowds needs either a four wheel drive vehicle, or will and stamina enough to walk. Fireplaces are officially provided at picnic spots to reduce the dangers of bushfires. Here the family prepare sizzling meals and the aroma of the gum trees is lost in blue smoke from burning steaks. Many suburban gardens have built-in barbecues which form a focus for summer evening parties.

Finally, a list of summer sports must include the ladies' bowling clubs, which abound and provide social meeting points.

SPORT IN WINTER

In winter sport lovers turn mainly to football, which, like cricket, also arrived shortly after the First Fleet. Four varieties are now played: rugby union, rugby league, 'Australian rules' and soccer. The fifteen-a-side rugby union dates from the 1880s and is most popular in the rural areas. The Australian team taking part in international Tests is known as the Wallabies; their most vigorous exchanges are with New Zealand. Rugby league has thirteen players; it is most popular in Queensland

I

and New South Wales and began as a breakaway group in 1907. The Australian team, the Kangaroos, take part in Test series, with sometimes over-enthusiastic spectator support.

Most exciting and popular of all is the version of rugby known as National Code, or more commonly just as 'Australian rules'. This is a uniquely Australian game deriving from an Irish game and from rugby. The first known game took place in the 1850s between two famous boys' schools in Melbourne when forty players a side dashed up and down between goal posts a mile apart. There is still some informality in the size and exact shape of the pitch, which is often making use of a cricket oval; the length can be from 150 to 250 yards. The main home of 'Aussie rules' is Melbourne, where it is followed with a near fanaticism. Four goal posts are aligned with the two central ones at least twenty feet high; a ball kicked between them scores six points, and a goal between the outer posts, called a 'behind', scores one point. There are no scrums, offsides or lineouts to slow or interrupt the game, which is played at high speed and demands tremendous athletic skill and stamina. The ball is not thrown; it can be punched or bounced along and must indeed be bounced at least every ten yards in the course of a player's run. High, leaping grabs or 'marks' distinguish the skilled player, cheered on by the crowd yelling 'Up! Up!' The shout of 'Up there, Cazaly' immortalised a Melbourne player by becoming a battle cry in both wars.

In recent years there has been a rapid growth in soccer which far surpasses both rugby codes and is now even threatening Australian rules in size of following. The game was brought more by European than British migrants; some club names like Prague or Budapest denote strong national groupings. British football pool promoters are glad of a source of competitions for their 'investors' to follow in the northern summer.

Golf is more readily accessible than in the more exclusive English atmosphere and is widely played. It is well endowed by commercial interests and prize money is often high. Australia has produced some top class international players in Peter Thompson and Kel Nagle, Norman von Nida and Bruce

Devlin. Joan Hammond of operatic fame was also a noted golfer.

Winter sports in the snows of the high country have increased very rapidly recently; a result of the improved access brought by the hydro-electric schemes and by the increasing affluence. The first Australian skiers were some gold seekers who kept themselves warm by organising races down the slopes at Kiandra in 1862. But the development of ski chalets and imitation alpine villages, of tow bars and chair lifts and the whole culture of ski and 'après ski' is quite recent. The enthusiast thinks nothing of the 300 mile drive from Sydney for a June weekend in the snows. He happily pays a small premium to ensure free transport for the forty miles to the nearest hospital at Cooma should he come to grief. The plateau slopes give good ski-ing conditions although below about 5,000ft there are the twisted trunks of the snow gums to negotiate.

Of the indoor winter sports, squash is also increasingly popular, and Australia has a world champion in Heather Mackay. Ten-pin bowling alleys have sprung up everywhere and are in use all year. Of the tougher pastimes, boxing, although still popular, is drawing rather less support than wrestling. There have been great boxing figures, from Les Darcy back in 1915 to Jimmy Carruthers in the 1950s and the recent champions Lionel Rose, a part Aborigine, and Johnny Famechon.

HORSE RACING

But of all the sports, horse racing leads the field by many lengths. In the world of racing, spectator is also speculator and the national love of gambling has full rein. There are over 4,000 race meetings a year; there are at least 180 clubs and 25,000 people professionally involved. The automatic totalisator was a New Zealand invention introduced to Australia in 1917. Flat racing is much more important than steeple chasing, which is more or less confined to South Australia and Victoria in the winter months. The racing season never ends, the venue simply shifts with the season. Spring and autumn meetings are held in Sydney rather earlier than in Melbourne with its longer wetter winter. Winter meetings are held in Brisbane and summer sees the horses, jockeys and their followings in Tasmania and Western Australia. There are many famous studs, notably in the Hunter valley of New South Wales; but not a few winners were bred in New Zealand. These include the now almost legendary *Phar Lap* (1926–32), whose abnormally large heart is pickled in a Canberra museum; his stuffed hide is displayed in Melbourne and his skeleton in New Zealand.

Totalisator 'investment' reaches well over $A600 million a year and has doubled since 1965. The day of the Melbourne Cup, held on the first Tuesday in November when the Victorian Racing Club runs a flat handicap over two miles, is a public holiday in Victoria. And it brings the rest of the nation to a standstill over the period of the race: civil servants gather in huddles, teachers retire conveniently to staff-rooms, while pupils may produce illicit radios and factory workers down tools to listen.

GAMBLING

Betting on horse racing accounts for about three-quarters of an estimated $A2,000 million spent on gambling every year in Australia. Following, but a very long way behind with a quarter of the total, comes the poker machine. Next come lotteries and the relatively small amounts that go on greyhounds and on footracing. The illegal 'two up' flourishes in the armed forces, in factories and among miners. Many Australian coal mines are situated in bushland which provides excellent cover for the 'schools'. The game simply comprises the tossing of two coins by the 'spinner' using a small wooden bat or 'kip'; bets are laid on the chances of both falling heads up. Lotteries are quite legal and indeed have the full blessing of authority, for the major organisers are the state governments of Queensland, New South Wales, Western and South Australia (the last only since 1967). Ticket sales exceed $A100 million a year and prizes are about two-thirds of the takings. The profits are in the main channelled into hospital funds and other charities. Lottery tickets sold by private concerns also bring in funds to the state from licensing fees. The biggest privately run lottery is Tattersalls', universally known as Tatts, which operates under state licence in Victoria and sells also in Tasmania and New Zealand. Tatts originated in Sydney but has also had its base in Queensland and for many years in Tasmania before being lured to Melbourne. There are lotteries run for charities, which are often called 'Art Unions' from an odd ancestry in the raffling of paintings in the last century. Probably the most famous of all lotteries is the one which provides funds for the Sydney Opera House; it is probably the only way the escalating costs of the building could have been met. Many people belong to small syndicates at office or club; it is all part of the national love of a gamble, which also leads many Australians into stock exchange speculation.

The poker machine is only legal in New South Wales, where it brings the government as much as $A14 million a year in licensing fees from over 20,000 of these 'one-armed bandits'. The huge profits go to the clubs running them for their members and finance amenities on a luxurious scale. Voices are sometimes raised against the poker machine and against the hold gambling has; but although there are cases of families deprived by addicted adults they are small in number and the gambling trends are not likely to decrease.

CLUBS

Membership of some sort of social club is common over a wide range of Australian society. Most clubs simply provide recreational facilities for sport, drinking or gambling. Membership is generally fairly easy to obtain; there are of course many with membership limited to specific groups. The biggest is the

RSL, the Returned Services League of Australia, which has branches in most centres of population and headquarters in Canberra. Membership, now over a quarter of a million, is confined to ex-servicemen who have served overseas or in specified parts of Northern Territory. The RSL is quite a powerful voice in the land and has statutory access to the cabinet. It is more akin to the American Legion than to the British Legion, and acts, according to its lights, as a sort of watch dog, following the motto 'The price of liberty is eternal vigilance.' This tends to make some of the utterances and pressures of the RSL take on a chauvinist and illiberal hue at times. The resentment aroused conceals the large amount of work the RSL does for its members in housing, employment and medical problems.

On a very different footing are the clubs offering some service to their community beyond a bar or poker machine. These include branches of international organisations like Rotary, and local groups of Apex or Lions Clubs. Specialised clubs are legion: a survey of those in Canberra revealed everything from a society for the growers of African violets to associations for Yugoslavs; from groups of sheepdog owners to pop groups; from amateur dramatics to the very worthy Police Boys' Clubs.

PAINTINGS

Paintings sell well in the affluent society, which is perhaps more concerned with their investment and prestige value than their intrinsic quality; but patronage of any sort provides some reward for the artist. There are five major and fourteen minor public art galleries and a growing number of private galleries. The National Gallery planned for a central site in Canberra is still at the preliminary stage of design; the emphasis in its collection will be on past and contemporary Australian art, and on Asian and Pacific art. The new Victorian Arts Centre in Melbourne is as sober and dignified as the Sydney Opera House is fanciful; its solid bluestone exterior encloses some very fine Australian workmanship, such as the magnificent roof of stained glass by Leonard French. The inland cities of Toowoomba in Queensland and Shepparton in Victoria have examples of good provincial galleries.

The Aborigines have a considerable artistic heritage which in part is being preserved though some say prostituted by the growing demand for tourist souvenirs. The bark paintings of Arnhem Land are widely recognised as being remarkable examples of a primitive art form; their detailed working includes both abstract design and accurate depiction of animals. Rock art was a widespread element in Aboriginal cultures, with many lively representations of the hunt, of human figures and of geometric patterns. Primitive Aboriginal art is much more exciting than the European styles of the group of talented painters gathered round Alice Springs, although their skill is admirable. The first and most famous of these was Albert Namtjira, whose facility was developed by Rex Batterbee. He was widely acclaimed and granted citizenship (of his own country!); this gave him drinking rights debarred at that time from his fellow Aborigines and when he shared drink with them, he was imprisoned; he died in 1959, a very disillusioned sacrifice to the clash of cultures.

European art arrived with the first settlers. At first English eyes could see only English things and the unique Australian landscapes were turned into babbling brooks and weeping willows. But this phase soon passed and more true renderings appeared. There were, for instance, vivid records of the goldfields by Gill. The first truly Australian group was the so-called Heidelberg School, named from the suburb of Melbourne where they lived in teaching camps around 1890. Its members included Roberts, Streeton and Condor and their subject matter captured some of the heat and light of Australia. The early twentieth century saw many Australian artists living and working overseas; and a spell of experience away from Australia has remained part of the pattern for many painters. The most successful painters of today are those who, having been influenced by modern trends, have none the less been able to apply their gifts and experience to their own environment. The results have included the harsh, near surrealist bush pictures of Tucker, Drysdale's grim pictures of the outback, Herman's urban scenes and William Dobell's memorable portraits. But most of all there is the genius of Sydney Nolan; his Ned Kelly series or the picture of the explorers Burke and Wills leaving Melbourne on their ill fated expedition of 1851 are clearly Australian. But his international reputation rests equally firmly on themes as far apart as classical Greece, timeless Antarctica, the Arizona deserts and the war spattered beaches of Gallipoli.

LITERATURE

Figures are produced to prove that Australians have more bookshops and buy more books per head than almost any other nation. But the high average conceals a large number who buy few or no books and a minority buying lavishly. Costs are high, with booksellers claiming to need a high 'mark up' to make a reasonable return. Publishing costs in Australia are high, and printing is now often undertaken in Japan or Hong Kong.

Library services were not good until quite recently. The self-educating movements based on Mechanics Institutes for instance brought to many towns a building still called School of Arts or such, but now without a book or picture in them. Library Boards and free subsidised libraries date from the 1930–50 period and are now well established. In Canberra the National Library has over a million volumes and over 15,000 films; some notable private collections of Australiana have been left to it. The public libraries of New South Wales and Victoria are first class, and those in other states of high standard. They were established in the nineteenth century, often in conjunction with museums and art galleries. In Sydney the Mitchell Library houses Australian material fundamental to any researcher, and university libraries are growing. School libraries have some subsidy from the Commonwealth but largely depend on the efforts of those stalwarts, the parents and citizens.

There are a fair number of Australian authors whose works enter the mainstream of world literature and are found in libraries throughout the English speaking world. Novelists range from H. H. Richardson, writing in the 1920s, to more modern writers like Patrick White and Thomas Keneally, who are still writing today. In the realms of popular fiction Jon Cleary and Morris West both produce very gripping best sellers, and Russell Braddon's books are full of sensitive insight. All three are widely read both in and outside Australia.

Poets of international repute include Kenneth Slessor and R. D. Fitzgerald writing earlier this century, and today, A. D. Hope commands a wide audience and has made successful journeys to the USA to read his astringent verse. Judith Wright, who lives on a Queensland property, is also well known overseas and at home for her poetry, which is sensitive, universal in its message, yet written from an unmistakably Australian background. The Commonwealth Literary Fund awards annual fellowships to allow promising or established writers to work full-time for a year; it also helps with publication costs in some cases.

THE PERFORMING ARTS

In the 1930s Australia was reputed to have the world's largest number of cinemas per head; but the bulk of the films shown in Australia were and are Hollywood imports. About sixty Australian sound films have been made, including *Jedda*, starring an Aboriginal actor Robert Tudawala whose later history sadly echoes that of Namatjira. The post-war trend to multi-million dollar spectaculars left the unsubsidised Australian film industry out of the running. But since 1967 about a dozen productions have been made in Australia, a number of them foreign or co-productions. The Commonwealth is now offering some financial help in promoting a Film Development Corporation, a National Film School and an Experimental Film Fund. There has been a continuous Australian contribution to film in the fine documentary work of the Commonwealth Film Unit. Chips Rafferty, the Australian actor, was widely known. As in other western countries, the cinema has had to compete with the rise of television; in Australia the consequent trend towards sensational violence and sex in filmmaking has had to contend with the strict censorship described at the end of this chapter. As in many of the drier and warmer parts of USA the 'drive in' open air cinema is very popular in Australia.

Live theatre performances draw good audiences on the whole, although the imported musical is perhaps more popular than indigenous serious theatre productions. The Australian Ballet and the Australian Opera have both made successful overseas tours; and of course Melba, Joan Sutherland, Joan Hammond and June Bronhill have become world famous singers. In the world of ballet, Sir Robert Helpmann is equally renowned and has returned to his own country to direct the biennial Adelaide Festival.

There is a strong demand for performed music although Australia has been slow to produce indigenous creative work in music of the stature say of a Nolan painting or a Patrick White novel. Permanent orchestras are maintained in the state capitals by the Australian Broadcasting Commission, which also sponsors concert series and invites artists from overseas. There are training facilities at Conservatories of Music, but still a severe lack of instrumentalists, and a relatively low number of orchestras in relation to population. The migrant influx has helped to vitalise the musical scene and there is emerging talent among young composers; the German born George Dreyfus is probably the only full-time professional composer; others of high repute are Sitzky, Meale and Sculthorpe. The major expatriate composer is Malcolm Williamson. The Australian Music Board, set up in 1967, advises the government on the production of Australian music at home and overseas.

Another word must be said about the Sydney Opera House to be opened in 1973. With the Harbour Bridge it is the first major Australian structure to meet the arrival by ship. Now all but complete, this fantastic creation of interlocking shells seems almost to float, like some spirit of the waves that dance and sparkle in one of the world's greatest harbours. The cultural equivalent in the post-war surge of enterprise which led to the Snowy Mountains Scheme, the Opera House was designed by the Danish architect Joern Utzon. Some of the revolutionary techniques needed to carry through his great concepts have been evolved through the engineering genius of Ove Arup. Utzon resigned as architect in 1966 after long and bitter controversy with the New South Wales Government. In the subsequent compromises the functional reason for the great shell vaults, designed to house the massive stage machinery needed for grand opera, has been lost; for the major hall will now be used only for concerts, and opera will be performed in the minor hall. There has been a lot of bitterness about the Opera House; but the chap who finances it through his lottery ticket is likely just to grin wryly and point out this great building with a mixture of pride and embarrassment to the visitor; he will visit it in due course but more probably to wander and ponder than to pine for the grand opera that never will be staged there.

HOLIDAYS AND FESTIVALS

The 25 April is a national holiday; this is Anzac Day, which commemorates the landings at Gallipoli by the Australian and New Zealand Army Corps in 1915. The unsuccessful Allied campaign, instigated by Winston Churchill, aimed to open a route to the grain lands of Russia and create a second front. It involved Indian, French and British troops as well as the Anzacs. But it was a baptism of fire for the colonial force, under which they first earned that redoubtable reputation as fighting men which they have justified again and again. By many Australians it was felt as the true birth of the nation. And on Anzac Day ceremonial marches take place following the very moving dawn service when the Last Post echoes through silent streets. Each year the ranks of the original Anzacs get thinner, the slim young RAAF pilots of the 1940s are more middle aged; the young Vietnam veterans swelled the numbers until Australian troops withdrew in 1971. Later in the day reunions become much less solemn affairs.

Australia Day on 26 January is also a national holiday, to celebrate the raising of the Union Jack by Captain Phillip at Sydney Cove in 1788. Commonwealth Day on 24 May was inaugurated in 1904 as Empire Day. It has become the traditional time for fireworks and bonfires. Guy Fawkes gets little attention on 5 November, a season of growing heat and bushfire danger. Labour Day is a holiday to mark the achievement of the eight hour working day, which goes back to 1871. It varies between the states: Tasmania, Western Australia and Victoria hold it in March, Queensland in May and New South Wales and South Australia in October. It is a time for picnics and rallies for workers and their families.

Other festivals are mainly local and linked with seasonal events. Some examples are the Banana Festival held in August in northern New South Wales, or the Apple Festivals in March in Tasmania and Western Australia. Grafton in New South Wales has its lovely Jacaranda Festival and Ballarat in Victoria a Begonia Festival. The wine growing valley of Barossa in South Australia has a Vintage Festival in April. Nearly all have fairs and carnivals. In Melbourne a two-week Moomba Festival was started in 1954; it takes place in March and includes book and art displays. Sydney has its Waratah Festival in October. The new Australians have brought some of their customs, adding colour and gaiety, for instance, to the weddings.

THE PRESS

The entire press is privately owned by an ever shrinking number of proprietors. Seven companies own or control the sixteen daily papers issued in the state capitals; there are nine morning and seven evening papers. (In the 1960s, three newspaper chains in Britain controlled 65 per cent of the daily and

Sunday press and in the USA 100 chains controlled a third of the 1,700 dailies. It is perhaps worth noting that the total of dailies in the world is about 6,500.) The same owners control most of the commercial television network. There are some thirty-five provincial papers, most of them weeklies and of strictly local relevance. Three-quarters of the papers printed belong either to the Melbourne based *Herald* and *Weekly Times* group or to the John Fairfax group in Sydney. Only *The Australian*, belonging to Rupert Murdoch, has a national circulation; started in Canberra, it now operates from Sydney with local editions.

The major Sydney and Melbourne dailies have a mass circulation because of the concentration of population in these two areas; the *Sydney Herald* and in Melbourne the *Age* circulate beyond the state boundaries in considerable numbers. There are no provincial centres large enough to support solid local dailies such as are the mainstay of US journalism. Nor is there anything to match the Olympian approach of the *Guardian* in Britain or the 'handsome and highminded *Christian Science Monitor*' (to quote *Encyclopaedia Britannica*) in the USA. The concentration of ownership is not entirely healthy even though most day to day decisions are left to the highly qualified editorial staff. The lack of alternative employers places journalists in an invidious position and some leave for other jobs or countries. Syndication of news both internal and by cable service is prevalent so that there is much uniformity in the way stories are presented. Oversea news is not very fully or rationally covered. The big dailies are preoccupied with the politics and sporting news of their own states. But although Australians have one of the highest rates of newspaper buying in the world, the general influence exerted is not in proportion.

There is not the marked contrast between the so called 'quality' papers as against the 'popular' press seen, say, in Britain and to some extent the USA. This probably reflects the small absolute numbers of people rather than a lack of demand for higher levels of journalism. Most papers try to cater for a very wide range so that high grade editorials and special articles are found along with a good deal of sport, comic strip and even astrology. The Saturday editions of the bigger papers carry both special articles and book reviews of a high standard. But there is no equivalent of the specialised *New York Book Review*.

The leading dailies are the conservative *Sydney Morning Herald* known by its fellows with a sort of affectionate disparagement as 'Granny', the *Age*, which is published in Melbourne and is almost equally staid, and the *Australian*. There is no paper supporting specifically Labor policies except possibly the union subsidised *Barrier Daily Truth* in the mining town of Broken Hill. The daily paper of the national capital is the *Canberra Times*, which blends national and international coverage with the local news of a community of some 144,000. Advertisements do not reach anything like American proportions save in the Saturday editions.

The weekly papers of comment comprise the slick and conservative *Bulletin*, a strange descendent from its radical nationalist and highly literate ancestor. There is the *Australian Financial Review* for the business community and the slim, articulate but unexciting *Nation* for the intellectuals. There are no equivalents of the American *New Republic* or the British *New Statesman*. Airmail editions of British papers find their way to a number of homes. The biggest selling journal is said to be the *Australian Women's Weekly*, taken by every second household. There are also the popular and pictorial *People* and *Pix*. At the other end of the intellectual gamut are literary quarterlies of very high standing: the more radical is *Meanjin* (an Aboriginal word meaning 'spike') and the more conservative *Quadrant*; both receive subsidies from the Commonwealth Literary Fund. There is plentiful specialist literature, but few periodicals for children are published in Australia.

RADIO AND TELEVISION

Television now claims the greatest attention as a source of leisure time amusement and interest and is blamed for any falling away of many live audiences whether from sport or symphony concerts. Both sound radio and television operate under a dual commercial and national system. The National Broadcasting System run by the Australian Broadcasting Commission, the ABC, had seventy-nine radio transmitting stations in 1969, of which twenty were in the state capitals. Many programmes are relayed from these to country stations and the capitals themselves are also linked to interchange material. The remote areas in the north and west are served by high frequency transmitters. The ABC was established by the Commonwealth government in 1932; its seven members are government appointed and must include at least one woman. They are chosen to represent as wide a range of interests as possible. Funds are derived direct from the Treasury and not through licensing fees as in Britain or exclusively from commercial sources as in the United States; so the degree of official involvement is high; and while the ABC maintains high standards there is some timidity in the field of critical appraisal. Proceedings in the House of Representatives must be broadcast; this can amuse, if unintentionally, but more often it dismays the listener, for the antics of politicians are seldom edifying in debate. The allocation of broadcasting time is a measure of the ABC's serious role: entertainment 28 per cent, classical music 24 per cent; news 9 per cent; the spoken word 7 per cent; sport 6 per cent; parliament 4 per cent; drama and features 4 per cent; education 4 per cent; light music 3 per cent; rural affairs 3 per cent; the balance is taken up by presentation (introduction, incidental music, etc).

Domestic programmes include serials, notably the long lived rural saga *Blue Hills*, and a number of others in the pattern familiar to British and American listeners to 'soap opera'. Radio Australia, aimed to project the Australian scene in south-east Asia, is the first programme the newcomer hears as the migrant ship steams towards Australian waters. The ABC has its own news gathering service and oversea correspondents. And it plays an important role in educational broadcasting. There is an excellent Kindergarten of the Air, and useful programmes to help migrants to adjust and to learn English.

The commercial radio stations are the antithesis of the ABC.

Local, not national, geared to pop music and not classical, to profit and not mental uplift, they are heavily indebted to imported material and to the disc jockey. There were 114 transmitting stations in 1969; broadcasters operate under five year licences issued by the Postmaster-General, who takes into account any recommendations made by the general overseeing body, the Broadcasting Control Board. It is perhaps scarcely surprising that surveys show approximately 75 per cent adherence to commercial against 25 per cent to ABC sound broadcasting. But local radio does play a very important part in such a large country. It provides a system for bush-fire warnings and can really save lives. Socially it allows openings for local news and comment, record requests, charity fund announcements as well as local advertising. The commercial stations are almost entirely owned by the local newspapers and in the capitals by bigger groups. The resurgence of radio in this transistor age is marked here as elsewhere, and very much in evidence in the outdoor living of the summer months.

The ABC also operates a National Television Service from thirty-nine stations (1969) and on a frequency of 625 lines; all but the most remote areas are served. Colour transmission will not begin until 1975, using the system developed in West Germany. There are forty-five commercial stations, again mainly in the hands of newspaper groups and the Ansett group. Both national and commercial systems are compelled by law to screen Australian made programmes for at least 50 per cent of their transmission time, with at least twelve hours a month in peak viewing hours. For the rest, USA provides three-quarters of the material and Britain the remainder. The ABC takes a higher proportion of British programmes, many of them comedy series like *Till Death Us Do Part*, but also dramatic serials including *The Forsyte Saga*. The commercial stations lean more to the American source. The Broadcasting Control Board sets limits for advertising time, but makes fewer stipulations on placing than in Britain, although there is more control than the USA has under the Federal Communications Commission; the resulting interruptions are bizarre at times. All television stations are obliged to put time at the disposal of religious bodies and political parties. Censorship of films for television is fairly strict.

CENSORSHIP

The vexed question of censorship is perhaps a sombre note on which to end a chapter on how the Australians amuse themselves; but it is of considerable significance to the cultural scene. Here the lurking puritanism, or 'wowserism' to quote their own term, still finds some expression. Australia has been placed in the same bracket with Portugal and Eire in the 'free world' in the degree of censorship. This perhaps overstates the case, but there are fairly restrictive attitudes.

The Minister of Customs and Excise is the final arbiter on all imported material, whether books or films. The states control material produced within their own borders, and the anomalies are considerable. The inter-state traffic in banned literature does sales nothing but good. In 1968 a National Literary Board was set up, including state and Commonwealth nominees, to act as a purely advisory body on the literary or artistic merit of works under review; this at least works towards more uniformity and might avoid some of the more ludicrous hold ups that result from the reactions of customs officers to titles on invoices. But the states reserve the right to prosecute even if titles are approved by the Board and by the Minister. And there is still too much interference in the acquisition of books of medical and psychological importance.

At the same time sex and violence portrayed on the paperback covers displayed at any bookstall are no more restrained than in any other western influenced country. Imported films are subject to censorship through the Film Censorship Board, which also acts for all the states save New South Wales and South Australia. Theatre productions are closely watched by the state authorities; in 1971 the entire cast of *Oh! Calcutta!* was temporarily arrested following the first Sydney performance. The paradoxes of the situation are endless and very Australian.

K

9

Hints for Visitors

TOURISTS visit Australia in increasing numbers every year. But it is a fairly expensive holiday from Europe or America, a once-in-a-lifetime experience that calls for care in planning. In 1972 spectacular reductions were announced on excursion fares by air which make it possible to have a month's stay for a very reasonable sum.

GETTING THERE

There are some forty shipping lines and fifteen major airlines serving Australia. And unless time is no object it is better to fly, at least part of the way. The flight from London is about thirty-six flying hours, and there are fifty to sixty flights a week from European airports. From the west coast of America it takes about twenty hours to Sydney. The strain of long flights, however, must not be underestimated, even given the attention to comfort that is a part of the service. Sleep is difficult save perhaps in the full luxury of first class travel. Light and loose clothing and travel slippers are a help, but a sweater and warm top coat should also be part of the cabin pack. The seasonal reversal of the southern hemisphere is worth emphasising again at the risk of stating the obvious, and at any time the traveller may strike cold spells. Travel by sea from Europe takes four to six weeks by South Africa and up to seven by Panama. From the west coast of North America the voyage is two to three weeks. Cost of sea travel from the USA to Sydney is disproportionately high compared with sea travel from Europe; this is because the passenger traffic from Europe is very much greater, and there is subsidisation of migrant travel which allows shipping companies to charge less to fare paying passengers.

All entail long periods at sea without landfall. While first class sea travel can be a holiday in itself, second or tourist class especially from Europe should be avoided unless everything has to be sacrificed for economy. Ships are often crowded by migrants so that meals involve several sittings; with young children it can be a nightmare. Boredom leads to heavy incidental expenditure which can whittle down savings made on the fare. On one class ships more expensive cabins are comfortable but public rooms are not; on two class ships segregation is severe.

A happy compromise lies in some of the combinations of sea and air journeys, notably the flight to Singapore followed by five days of sea travel to Fremantle. Some freighters like Blue Star Line and some Scandinavian lines still carry a few passengers and are for the adult with plenty of time, good health and a capacity for reading. Then there are overland trips for the intrepid, getting the traveller as far as India and south-east Asia, from where he can continue by air or sea.

GETTING IN

Since Australia is a member of the British Commonwealth of Nations a British or British Commonwealth passport, provided the holder is of 'European' origin, is almost an Open Sesame, if combined with international travel documents relating to health. All other passport holders need a visa which is usually valid for six months. This is issued to *bona fide* travellers, who must prove, however, that in Australia they can support themselves or be supported by an Australian resident. They must also have a return ticket and undertake not to seek any employment in Australia. The visa is cancelled on arrival and replaced by an Entry Permit also valid for six months, with extensions available up to twelve months; this applies to British passport holders also. Non-European holders of British passports must obtain an Endorsement Voucher in order to stay and this has the same conditions attached to it as a visa. Working holiday permits are available to US citizens of European race who are under thirty and have been granted a visa. There are also student permits valid up to twelve months and renewable. A valid international health card must show duly certified small-pox vaccination; and travellers from areas of endemic cholera (mainly south and south-east Asia) must be inoculated, as must those from areas with yellow fever, such as some African countries. The smallpox certificate may be waived for babies under a year, and on medical or religious grounds for sea travellers only. Visitors staying over six months must have a chest X-ray in Australia, before continuing their stay.

Before the ship or plane arrives passengers are given customs declarations to complete. Regulations are generous in relation to genuinely personal possessions, including cameras, tape recorders and so on; in general firearms cannot be taken in. A duty free allowance of 400 cigarettes, 1½lb of tobacco and half a gallon of spirits can be taken ashore. Apart from these, gifts not exceeding $A100 in value are allowed. Australian customs officials are generally relaxed and courteous, but they keep a stern and watchful eye for two dangers. One is any possible disease of plant, animal or human that may be inadvertently introduced. The dreaded 'foot and mouth' disease that affects European stock has so far been kept out of Australia, and its introduction could be disastrous. Quarantine regulations are strict in respect of humans too. The second danger is the possible introduction of alleged moral contamination in the form of literature or films, as explained on p 153. It is better to be very conservative in the books you have with you to avoid at best infuriating delays.

GETTING ON

Australians are easy to get on with, at least at the superficial level, provided a few points are remembered. Although there are in fact quite steep social gradients within the community, the general belief that 'Jack's as good as his master' rules out any form of exchange that implies superiority on the one hand and subservience on the other. This leads to extreme informality in personal services, and a general lack of help in carrying bags, calling taxis and so on. The taxi driver expects a single passenger to get in beside him; the visitor will then be treated to as much information as he wants. He should on no account proffer a tip for that would give offence; and this goes for all personal service.

Australians are proud of their country, and they are naturally edgy about any critical comment. In his book *Australia* (1968), O. H. K. Spate, an Englishman happily settled in Australia, divided visitors into two categories: those who give press interviews extolling the dynamic youth of this great land of opportunity, and those who go home and write books decrying the materialist culture but praising the hospitality; both types tend to be patronising. It is not necessary to be either to enjoy a very happy visit, if the visitor guards his tongue and reserves his judgements.

GETTING ABOUT

Avoid Australia at the height of summer (January–March) save perhaps for Tasmania. Even the equable coastal areas are uncomfortably hot, at least for people from temperate latitudes. Most Australians have their summer break at that time anyway and resorts are crowded. Away from the coast bush flies are rampant in shady spots; they are not disease carrying but are a terrible nuisance, and they lead to that characteristic 'Australian swipe' as one brushes them away from the face; they are guaranteed to ruin any picnic. Mosquitoes take over the night shift near any water; they do not transmit malaria but can bite viciously.

The dangers of sharks and snakes are far smaller than the dangers of road travel. But bush walkers should wear protective clothing and never explore too closely round or under fallen tree trunks. Antidotes for all known snake bites are widely held in hospitals but some description is invaluable to identify the species. Snakes are seldom aggressive unless they or their young are threatened. A tourniquet between the bite and the heart is the first measure of help, releasing it at one minute intervals. A snake can be whipped up under a car bonnet; treat him as alive until it is certain he is not. But most visitors, like most Australians, will never so much as see a snake. There are a few poisonous spiders: the funnel web of the humid south-east sometimes invades bathrooms, and the tiny redback of the interior can be serious for a small child.

The motorist may come on kangaroos along bush roads at dusk, when they are hard to see. The number of dead animals along the wayside is a measure of the problem. But his greatest risk is from his fellow drivers. Seat belts are fitted and in most states of Australia it is now illegal not to have them fastened; a reform already showing results in lower accident figures. Sand or soil drifts across roads should be taken slowly in low gear, so should floodwaters, which can rise very rapidly. Really outback roads are only for the experienced. The motoring associations keep records of weather and road conditions and will advise on routes and maps, though the latter are of varying accuracy on the existence or otherwise of roads. An international driving permit will cover variations in licensing laws between the states. If tempted into rough country it is wise always to leave destinations and estimated time of arrival with the police; and if the car breaks down, never wander away from it.

On the whole tourists stay on the beaten track, which in the nature of things will take them to most of the scenic wonders of the continent. Internal air travel combined with bus or car hire covers most ground when time is limited. Rail fares are cheaper than air, but rather complex in booking arrangements and of varying comfort. The Barrier Reef is reached by launch services from Queensland ports like Cairns, Mackay and Gladstone. There are also flights to and over some of the islands. The National Parks throughout the country cover a wide range of landscape from rain forest to desert, and of wild life from koalas to kangaroos. It is better to visit Queensland and the centre of the continent in 'winter', which in fact is dry and warmer than most English summers, although not those of USA for the most part. In the Centre the visitor can stay at a cattle station, fossick for gold and of course visit Ayers Rock; the burning colours of the rocks are unforgettable. For the west and south of the country, spring and autumn are better.

A possible four to six months' itinerary might begin about March or April (autumn) with arrival at Perth by sea or air. The *Indian Pacific* (booked well in advance) will carry the traveller in air-conditioned luxury a 70 hour journey east to Sydney. Several weeks can be easily filled from Sydney as a base: the coast, the cliffs and waterfalls of the Blue Mountains, Canberra and the Snowy Mountains (which may already have a sprinkling of white) are easily accessible. A journey north to Queensland would take in the rain forest and the Barrier Reef, with perhaps a journey by train or plane to the cattle country of the interior—exhausting but very instructive. By June the time has come to fly into the Centre and take coach trips from Alice Springs. Motoring becomes more possible at this time, though distances are long, for example, up the Stuart Highway to Darwin. There is no good road south from Alice Springs; here the *Ghan* train takes people and vehicles.

As spring begins to break in the south a return to Sydney could be followed by taking the Princes Highway round the coast to Melbourne, which passes through some industrial landscapes in both New South Wales and Victoria. An off season journey to Tasmania might catch the apple blossom; or a drive can be taken north-west to see the vineyards, or north through the hills to the Murray valley pastures and orchards. To the west, the Flinders Ranges of South Australia have lovely wild flowers, and Adelaide possesses a unique charm. But try to catch the wild flower season of Western Australia in October to December; it is a great glory. And if time and money (and stamina) are still holding out, take a flight north to look at the vast iron fields and new towns of the Pilbara, and even to the very far north-west to the remote Kimberleys. Such a journey would leave a feast of memories, and some impressions at least of the size and character of the unique continent.

Acknowledgements

THE author would like to express her sincere thanks to the following: Frederick Warne & Co Ltd for permission to make use of her previous work in *Encyclopaedia of Australia*; Chatto & Windus Ltd for permission to include the quotation on p 59; Dr Godfrey Linge of the Department of Human Geography, Australian National University, Canberra, for sending the results of the 1971 census immediately they were printed; and John Hunt of the Britain's Open University for drawing the map.

The following books have been invaluable sources: HRH the Duke of Edinburgh's Third Commonwealth Study Conference, *Anatomy of Australia* (Melbourne 1968); P. H. Partridge, *Society Schools and Progress in Australia* (Oxford 1968); Geoffrey Sawer, *Australian Government Today* (Melbourne 1967); and O. H. K. Spate, *Australia* (London 1968).

Jacket illustration: Australian beef cattle returning from summer pastures near the Victorian section of the Australian Alps. Courtesy of the Australian news and information service.

Index

Aborigines, 15, 17–20, 25, 27, 38, 62, 66, 67, 81, 82, 83, 93, 95–6, 136, 139, 143
Accidents, motor, 83, 129
Adelaide, 63–4, 76, 96
Animals,
  introduced, 15
  native, 14–15
Anzac Day, 147–8
Asians in Australia, 23–4, 56
Australia, the name of, 9
Australian Broadcasting Commission, 151–2
Australian Labor Party (ALP), 22, 23–4, 30, 38, 50, 65, 87
Australian Rules football, 61, 137, 138
Australia Party, 54
Aviation, 87, 124–6
Ayers Rock, 12–13, 159

Ballet, 146
Banking, 46, 87
Bauxite, 19, 93
Boomerangs, 17
Boxing, 139
Bradman, Sir Donald, 136
Brisbane, 42, 62, 76, 89, 90, 129

Broken Hill Proprietary Company Ltd (BHP), 91, 130

Canberra, 67–8, 75–6
Cars, 96, 124, 129, 158
Cattle industry, 19, 67, 97–9
Censorship, 35, 62, 146, 153–4, 156
Chinese in Australia, 21, 67
Climate, 11–12
Clothing, 78–9, 96, 154
Clubs, social, 141–2
Common Market, 99, 100
Commonwealth of Australia, composition of, 9
Communist Party, 38, 54
Conscription, 55
Conservation, 16, 17, 95
Constitution of the Commonwealth, 19, 35, 37, 39, 48, 128
Convicts, 20–1, 28, 62, 63, 65, 66, 74, 128
Cook, Captain James, 26
Copper, 93, 110, 127
Country Party, 30, 41, 50, 53, 61, 65
Cricket, 136–7
Currency, 10, 39, 46–7

Customs and excise, 39, 156

Darwin, 30, 67
Defence, 35, 39, 55–6
Democratic Labor Party (DLP), 54, 61
Discovery of Australia, 26
Divorce, 48

Education, 35, 112–23
  independent schools, 116–17
  primary schools, 115
  secondary schools, 115–16
  technical, 121–2
  tertiary, 117–22
  universities, 118–21
Entry to Australia, 155–6
Electricity, 72, 73, 88, 89–90
Examinations, 118
Explorers, 13, 27

Federation, 29
Films, 75, 145–6, 153
Flying Doctor Service, 82, 97
Food, 77–8
Foreign aid, 56
Foreign policy, 56–7

Gambling, 140–1
Gold, 12, 21, 28, 60, 94
Golf, 138–9
Governor General, 36, 37
Governors, 27, 39
Great Artesian Basin, 14
Great Barrier Reef, 16, 159
Great Dividing Range, 13
Greeks in Australia, 77

High Court of Australia, 37–8, 47, 48

Hobart, 66, 72, 76
Holidays, 147–8
Horse racing, 139–40
House of Representatives, 35–6
Housing, 70–4

Income tax, 35, 38, 45, 113
Industrial relations, 39, 101–2
Industry, 87–97
Inflation, 102, 105–6, 107
Innovations,
  mechanical, 25
  political, 29, 40
Irish in Australia, 21, 54, 114
Iron and steel industry, 91–2
Iron ore, 12, 63, 64, 91, 92, 110, 160
Italians in Australia, 62, 77

Japan, Australian relations with, 30, 57, 92, 108–9, 110, 131

Kangaroos, 14, 16, 158
Koalas, 14, 16

Language, 25
Lead, 93, 110
Legal system, 47–9
Legislative Assemblies, 39
Legislative Councils, 40
Liberal/Country Party Coalition, 30, 38, 60, 87, 115
Liberal Party, 30, 50, 54
Libraries, 144
Life Saving Clubs, 134–5
Loan Council, 44
Local government, 39, 42

Means test, 79, 80, 119

Melbourne, 61, 72, 76, 90, 96, 129

Melbourne Cup, 140

Menzies, Sir Robert, 50, 56

Merino sheep, 27

Migration, 20, 22–3, 30

Minerals, 31, 88–96

Murray-Darling River, 14, 100

Music, 146

Namatjira, Albert, 143

National Parks, 16, 159

Natural gas, 63, 73, 88, 90–1

Newspapers, 148–50, 152

Nickel, 12, 94

Nolan, Sydney, 144

Northern development, 98–9

Novelists, 145

Nuclear power, 90

Oil, 88, 90–1

Opals, 63

Opera, 146

Painting, 20, 142–3

Papua-New Guinea, 56, 68–9

Periodicals, 150

Perth, 65, 71–2, 76, 92

Plants,
  introduced, 15
  native, 15–16

Poets, 145

Police, 35, 49

Political parties, 36–7, 50–5

Population, 24, 28, 58

Poverty, 79

Premiers' Conference, 44, 110

Privy Council, 38, 48

Public health, 82–3

Public service, 43

QANTAS, 124–5

Radio, 97, 113, 151–2

Railways, 29, 44, 62, 126–8, 159

Referenda, 19, 38, 55

Religion, 24–5

Roads, 128–9

Rugby football, 137–8

Sailing, 135

Schools of the Air, 113

Senate, 35, 36, 37, 54

Settlement of Australia, 20, 28–9

Sharks, 133–4, 158

Shipbuilding, 130–1

Shipping, 87, 130–1, 154

Skiing, 139

Snakes, 15, 158

Snowy Mountains, 13, 31, 59, 67, 89–90

Soccer, 138

Sport, 132–40

Squash, 139

Squatters, 27, 28, 62

Strikes, 105, 106

Sugar, 99–100

Swimming, 133, 135

Sydney, 59–60, 72, 74, 76, 96, 121

Sydney Opera House, 141, 146–7

Tariffs, 108

Television, 149, 150–1

Tennis, 135–6

Territories,
  external, 9, 68–9
  internal, 9, 28, 32, 58, 66–8

Trade, 108–9

Trade Unions, 29, 101, 106

Unemployment, 84, 107, 108, 110
United Nations, 56
Uranium, 93–4
United States, Australian links with, 23, 30, 57, 109

Vietnam War, 30, 57
Voting, 19, 35–6, 40–1

War Memorial, National, 56
Welfare, 79–83
Wheat, 29, 61, 63, 64, 97, 99
White Australia policy, 21, 22, 23–4
Wine, 78, 100
Women at work, 106–7
Woomera, 63
Wool, 27–8, 63, 64, 97, 98
World Wars, 30